Forms that Work

The Morgan Kaufmann Series in Interactive Technologies

Measuring the User Experience: Collecting, Analyzing, and Presenting Usability Metrics
Tom Tullis and Bill Albert

Moderating Usability Tests: Principles and Practices for Interacting
Joseph Dumas and Beth Loring

Keeping Found Things Found: The Study and Practice of Personal Information Management
William Jones

GUI Bloopers 2.0: Common User Interface Design Don'ts and Dos
Jeff Johnson

Visual Thinking for Design
Colin Ware

User-Centered Design Stories: Real-World UCD Case Studies
Carol Righi and Janice James

Sketching User Experiences: Getting the Design Right and the Right Design
Bill Buxton

Text Entry Systems: Mobility, Accessibility, Universality
Scott MacKenzie and Kumiko Tanaka-ishi

Letting Go of the Words: Writing Web Content that Works
Janice (Ginny) Redish

Personas and User Archetypes: A Field Guide for Interaction Designers
Jonathan Pruitt and Tamara Adlin

Cost-Justifying Usability
Edited by Randolph Bias and Deborah Mayhew

User Interface Design and Evaluation
Debbie Stone, Caroline Jarrett, Mark Woodroffe, and Shailey Minocha

Rapid Contextual Design
Karen Holtzblatt, Jessamyn Burns Wendell, and Shelley Wood

Voice Interaction Design: Crafting the New Conversational Speech Systems
Randy Allen Harris

Understanding Users: A Practical Guide to User Requirements: Methods, Tools, and Techniques
Catherine Courage and Kathy Baxter

The Web Application Design Handbook: Best Practices for Web-Based Software
Susan Fowler and Victor Stanwick

The Mobile Connection: The Cell Phone's Impact on Society
Richard Ling

Information Visualization: Perception for Design, 2nd Edition
Colin Ware

Interaction Design for Complex Problem Solving: Developing Useful and Usable Software
Barbara Mirel

The Craft of Information Visualization: Readings and Reflections
Written and edited by Ben Bederson and Ben Shneiderman

HCI Models, Theories, and Frameworks: Towards a Multidisciplinary Science
Edited by John M. Carroll

Web Bloopers: 60 Common Web Design Mistakes, and How to Avoid Them
Jeff Johnson

Observing the User Experience: A Practitioner's Guide to User Research
Mike Kuniavsky

Paper Prototyping: The Fast and Easy Way to Design and Refine User Interfaces
Carolyn Snyder

Forms that Work

Designing Web Forms for Usability

Caroline Jarrett

Gerry Gaffney

ELSEVIER

AMSTERDAM • BOSTON • HEIDELBERG • LONDON
NEW YORK • OXFORD • PARIS • SAN DIEGO
SAN FRANCISCO • SINGAPORE • SYDNEY • TOKYO
Morgan Kaufmann Publishers is an imprint of Elsevier

Morgan Kaufmann Publishers is an imprint of Elsevier.
30 Corporate Drive, Suite 400, Burlington, MA 01803, USA
This book is printed on acid-free paper.

Library of Congress Cataloging-in-Publication Data
Application Submitted

ISBN: 978-1-55860-710-1

Typeset by Charon Tec Ltd., A Macmillan Company.
(www.macmillansolutions.com)

For information on all Morgan Kaufmann publications,
visit our Web site at www.mkp.com or www.elsevierdirect.com

Printed in China

11 12 13 14 15 16 5 4 3 2

Contents

Interlude: Registration forms: What to do if you can't avoid them

Case study: A conference booking form: A sample question protocol

Interlude: Serif or sans serif font?

Case study: A makeover

In the beginning—dozens of years ago—research papers crawled out of the primordial ooze somewhere in Switzerland to form the World Wide Web.

People in university basements posted the papers, and people in other university basements around the world could read them. Read-only.

Then one day someone in one of the basements thought, "Wait. Why couldn't the people who *read* these things *send* us information, too?" And thus < form > < /form > was born.

And although no one knew it at the time, e-commerce was born, too, because as Caroline and Gerry explain in the pages you're about to read, forms enable a *conversation* between Web publisher and Web user. It was such a powerful and useful idea that there's hardly a site today that doesn't have a form...or dozens of forms.

And since we've all used forms all of our lives[1], we know just how unpleasant bad forms can be:

- Forms that ask questions you don't know how to answer
- Forms with multiple-choice questions that don't have the choice you want
- Forms that ask for too much information, or information you'd rather not give
- Forms with huge quantities of confusing instructions

...and on and on.

In an ordinary conversation, we work these things out by asking for and offering clarifications ("Do you mean my average income *lately*, or for my whole life?" "How many children do I *have*, or how many are living at home?"). But since a form can only ask the questions we tell it to ask, in exactly the way we tell it to ask them, a *good* form has to be completely clear and completely self-explanatory. That's where this book comes in.

[1]Some of us are even old enough to remember multi-part carbon paper forms, with instructions like "Press hard! You are making seven copies."

I've known Caroline Jarrett for a long time, and she's always been one of my favorite people in this usability racket.[2] It's not just that I like her personally (although she is, as we'd say over here, a really good egg); it's that she's one of the handful of people whose opinions about usability I always want to hear.

And I've always thought of her as *the* Web forms expert—someone who can talk for an hour about whether to use colons at the end of labels and make it interesting (although she'd insist that it's not, except to people like her who are obsessed with forms).

But this book isn't just about colons and choosing the right widgets. It's about the whole process of making good forms, which has a lot more to do with making sure you're asking the right questions in a way that your users can answer than it does with whether you use a drop-down list or radio buttons.

Like a conversation with Caroline, this book she and Gerry have done gets to the heart of the matter. It's long on practical advice, extremely generous in sharing their vast experience, and full of exactly the advice you need.

I'm lucky. When I have a question about forms, I can just check to see if Caroline has Skype on, or send her an email. Now you're almost as lucky: you've got the next best thing in your hands.

Steve Krug
Brookline, Massachusetts
April 2008

[2]I've never met Gerry in person, mostly because he lives halfway round the world with all those koalas, dingoes, and hobbits. (No, wait. The hobbits are New Zealand.) But I know from Caroline—and from the way this book turned out—that he's top notch, too. However they divided the labor, it worked.

Acknowledgements

This book took a long time to write, and many people helped us along the way. We'd like to thank the clients who let us experiment with them—trying out our ideas, and allowing us to recruit their customers and users to test their forms. Watching a user work on your form is the single best way to find out about it. Discussing the problems you find with a client runs pretty close. Outstanding amongst them was Christine Huddlestone of HM Revenue and Customs, who worked so hard to get usability into UK tax forms. Together, we convinced John Willmer, Head of Forms for HM Revenue and Customs, to back our ideas—the origins of many in this book.

Another great way of learning for us has been through teaching forms design—and having many enjoyable arguments with people who have attended tutorials. We'd like to thank everyone who has commissioned or been part of these training sessions, especially Jakob Nielsen, Nick Jones of Nationwide Building Society, Jackie Stuart of the Australian Taxation Office, Gian Sampson-Wild of Monash University, and Denise Fayne, George Freeland, and Bob Erickson of the IRS.

Many dear friends and colleagues suffered through multiple drafts of this material, generously commenting and encouraging, even when it looked like it might never be finished. Christine Elgood was the first to tackle the problem of helping us to turn vague thoughts into concrete words; Debbie Stone worked on so many versions that she must have lost count; Ginny Redish and Steve Krug stole unreasonable amounts of time from their own books to help this one along; Whitney Quesenbery listened to a lot and read drafts in a hurry.

And there's a long, distinguished roll-call of friends, colleagues and clients who commented, offered examples, shared experiences or spotted mistakes. We hope we've remembered most of you; we thank all of you; we're sorry that many great things didn't make it into this final version: Dey Alexander, Mark Barratt, Michael Barlow, Mary Beth Rettger, Rusty Boehm, Rob Burnside, Giles Colborne, Barry Day, Annie Drynan, Brent Emerson, Jessica Enders, Susan Farrell, David Halbig, Richard Ishida, Beth Mazur, Sue MacLeod, Bret Pettichord, Scott Rippon, Joseph Seeley, Derek Sisson, Kevin Sleeman, Carolyn Snyder, Donna (Maurer) Spencer, Andrew Starling, Daniel Szuc, Howard Tamler, Margaret Tassin, Jim Thatcher, Michael Thornhill, Manabu Ueno,

Jeff Veen, Howard Wells, Jo Wong, Pat Wright, Fiz Yasdi, Carl Zetie, Daniel Szuc.

Diane Cerra originally signed this book and believed in us; Denise Penrose, Mary James and Melinda Ritchie saw it through to completion.

And finally, thanks to Gina Ellis for all her help and support, to Malcolm Jarrett for advice on beer, to Brian Gaffney for his help with sourcing examples, and to Marcus Gaffney for the hugs.

Caroline Jarrett

Caroline Jarrett was a project manager specialising in Optical Character Recognition when she landed a job delivering OCR systems to the UK Inland Revenue for processing tax forms. The systems didn't work and she found out that it was because of the way people filled out the forms. She became fascinated with the problem of how to design forms so that people find them easy to use—a fascination that shows no signs of wearing off, 15 years later.

Caroline runs the usability consulting company Effortmark Ltd in Leighton Buzzard, UK. She writes a monthly column "Caroline's Corner' on www.usabilitynews.com.

Gerry Gaffney

Gerry Gaffney has always had a fear of forms. He met Caroline while looking for ways to help clients design better forms. She persuaded him that a dispassionate point of view about forms was essential to this book. Gerry remains strangely resistant to Caroline's obsession with forms, but is glad that someone cares that much.

Gerry runs the usability consulting company Information & Design in Melbourne, Australia. He was Managing Editor of User Experience magazine in 07/08, and he also produces the popular User Experience Podcast (uxpod.com).

The cartoons on pages xv, 16, 34, 36, 50, 58, 72, 93, 95, 174 and 178 are copyright of and used with permission from Effortmark Ltd.

The photograph of the Florida 'Butterfly Ballot' on page 2 is copyright of and used with permission from Steve Krug.

The cartoon on page 24 is copyright of and used with permission from Graeme MacKay.

The image on page 66 is used with permission of Ricky Buchanan and No Pity T-shirts. http://nopityshirts.com

The "OK/Cancel" cartoon strip on page 88 is copyright of and used with permission from Kevin Cheng.

The cartoon on page 112 is copyright of and used with permission from www.CartoonStock.com.

The photograph of a usability test on page 178 is copyright of and used with permission from Effortmark Limited and also with permission of the people in the picture.

The cartoon on page 183 is copyright of and used with permission from Information & Design Pty. Ltd.

Introduction:
What is a form?

Why forms matter

Forms are everywhere. Most of us will fill in at least one form every day: logging on at work, filling in time sheets, signing for credit card purchases. Major events in our lives have forms associated with them, from the birth register filled in by the nurse or midwife when we are born to marriage certificates, passport applications, and voter registrations.

Bad forms can have serious consequences

Hoffmann, Zimmerman, and Tompkins, 1996

A poor form can have nasty consequences. One study looked at "living wills," the forms that patients fill in to instruct their doctors about whether they want medical treatment if they can no longer decide for themselves—for example, if in a persistent vegetative state. Of the completed forms, 41% gave contradictory instructions, and a similar number did not correctly describe the intentions of the people who filled them in.

Occasionally, a form will be so bad that it makes headlines. No book on forms could ignore the "butterfly ballot," the election form that confused voters in Florida in 2000 and had a pivotal effect on the U.S. presidential election. Some voters said that they had voted for Pat Buchanan, a minority candidate and the second hole down in punch order, when they had intended to vote for Al Gore, the Democratic candidate and the second ticket down on the left of the ballot in reading order.

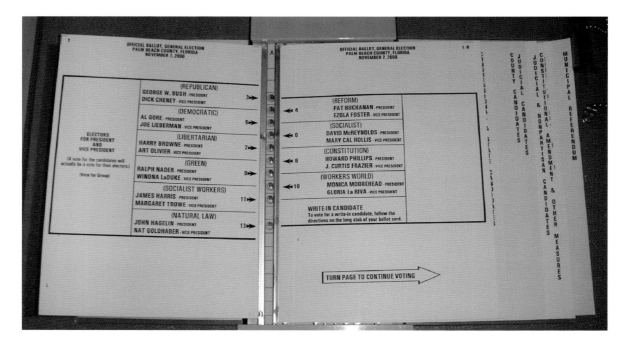

Good forms create good experiences

A good form can provide a good service. When the web was new, it was exciting merely to offer a few pages of information to the visitor. The early versions of HTML did not include tags for forms. But gradually, people wanted to do things on the web as well as view information.

Forms started to appear. At first, they were hidden in the backwaters of websites. Now they are everywhere. Everyone uses Google—a home page that's really just a form.

Some websites are crammed with forms. Continental Airlines has five on its home page: to book a flight, print a boarding pass, change a reservation, log in as frequent flyer, and search. These forms let you do things straight away.

What this book is about

We like good forms, and we don't like bad ones. So this book is about how to design good forms and how to avoid design mistakes.

It's about design, not technology

The people filling in the forms, known to us as *users* of the forms, don't change that much. Over the past few years, we've noticed them:

- get a bit more confident, more willing to buy things on the Web;
- get a bit more protective, less willing to reveal personal information;
- get a bit more demanding, less willing to tolerate bad forms.

But mostly, they continue to react to forms just as they always did.

The technologies available, however, change rather rapidly. We also find that for most forms projects, someone else chooses the technology and we have to live with it.

So this book is about design. There's almost no technology in it.

It's about the Web, not paper

We love paper. We've been working with paper for years. We wanted to put lots and lots of great thoughts about paper forms in this book.

Then we looked at it and thought: That book is too long.

So this book is about the Web. But if you're working on paper forms (or some other medium), you'll find many of the ideas are helpful.

It's about usability: making forms easier to use

Underlying everything in this book is that it's about *usability*—the quality of being easy to use. We assume that you're here because you, too, want to design your forms to be easy to use. For us, it's become a passion.

It's got a process in it: try it, you might like it

Life isn't always orderly. We've included a "messy and typical process" with some pointers to how this book might help you with it. If you can, try the orderly process that follows the organization of the book. From time to time, we get the chance to start at the beginning of the orderly process and continue through to the end—and we're always delighted to find that it really does work.

Some definitions and two processes

We thought we should start with definitions.

You know a form when you see it

A *form* is a web page that has boxes you can type into.

You might say it's also a form if you can click radio buttons or choose from drop-downs. But it's the "field for me to type into" that really makes the difference.

Definition

Mostly, people don't worry about the formal definitions. They know a form when they see one. Look at these two screenshots. They are deliberately too small to read. Even at a glance, you can immediately identify the one that is a form: it's the one with the fields to type into.

The three layers: relationship, conversation, and appearance

If forms are just web pages with boxes that you can type into, why don't people like them?

We've done a lot of work on government forms, and we've noticed that people don't like them before they've even seen them. They don't even like the idea of having to tackle forms. This is a problem with the relationship between the individual and the task imposed by the form.

Then they sit down and try it. And they find that it's hard going—difficult to understand and hard to know whether they have put the correct answers. The conversation isn't going smoothly.

And on top of all that, government forms are often very ugly. The appearance is poor.

We've found that we could make the forms look a lot better, but that didn't help people to understand them. We sorted out the language used in the forms and made them ask questions that people understood and could answer, but they still considered that filling out government forms wasn't going to be an enjoyable part of their day.

The three layers of the form were first published in Jarrett (2000).

So we constructed our theory of the three layers of the form: **relationship**, **conversation,** and **appearance**.

The *relationship* of a form is the relationship between the organization that is asking the questions and the person who is answering.

The *conversation* of a form comes from the questions that it asks, any other instructions, and the way the form is arranged into topics.

The *appearance* of a form is the way that it looks: the arrangement of text, input areas such as fields and graphics, and the use of color.

Throughout this book we'll come back to these three layers of the form: We'll discuss them in detail, separately, so they may start to feel like separate issues, but in forms design the three layers are interdependent. The person filling in the form will experience all the layers together, so they all have to work well.

And above all, you get a good form by testing it with users—and then doing something about what you learn in the test.

A messy but typical forms design process

In our experience most forms get designed in a process rather like this one—if they get any design attention at all. Some forms seem to go directly from "First draft appears" to "Launch it—no time for testing" without any intervening improvement.

Other times, while we're trying not to forget the people (users) who will use the forms, somehow the users aren't really in focus. The challenges of working with the stakeholders, writing the questions, organizing them into a logical flow, and then keeping the layout in order are more immediate.

If you are forced into such a process, usually because of lack of time, we hope that the ideas in this book will help you to produce something that at least tries to be a good form that works well for your users. Most of what we say is relatively obvious in hindsight and, once you know it, you should find that it takes no longer to create a really good, usable form than it does to create a badly designed one.

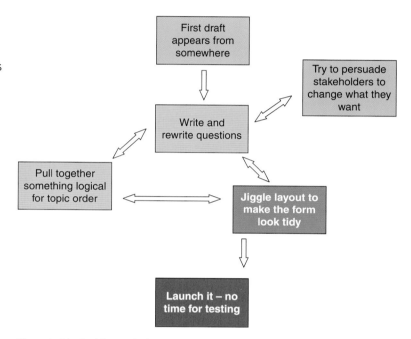

Messy but typical forms design process. It's hard to remember the people who use the forms when there are so many other things to do.

When you're working on your first draft and trying to persuade your stakeholders, look in Chapters 1 and 2, on relationship, for some ideas.

When you start writing questions, Chapters 3 to 6 on conversation should give you some ideas.

Arguing about details, like whether to put a colon at the end of your labels? That's what Chapter 7, the first part of appearance, is for.

Jiggling layout? Then try Chapter 8, the other half of appearance: Making the form look easy.

And, even if you think you have no time for testing, try Chapter 9. You can test your form in half an hour. Surely you've got time for that?

The methodical design process that really works

We really want you to try the methodical design process, to start from the beginning and work through in the same order as the book.

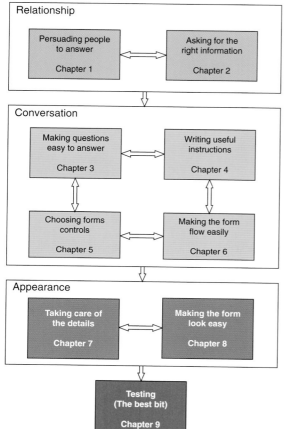

The success of your form hinges on persuading people to answer the questions on the form, preferably accurately. So we start with "who" in Chapter 1, "Persuading People to Answer." We look at who answers and why they might do so. It's the first half of the relationship layer.

In Chapter 2, "Asking for the Right Information," we answer the other questions: what, where, when, and why. We look at what the organization wants to achieve with the form.

Chapters 3 to 6 are all about the conversation layer:

- Having got people into the right mood to answer, how can you ask questions in the best way? Chapter 3, "Making Questions Easy to Answer," starts with our ideas about how questions work and has suggestions for writing good questions for your forms.

- Sometimes you need extra words to explain concepts on the form. If so, read Chapter 4, "Writing Useful Instructions."

- In Chapter 5, "Choosing Forms Controls," we look at how to choose the right web control to use for each question.

- One of the advantages of forms on the web, and electronic forms in general, is that you can guide people through the process of filling them in. In Chapter 6, "Making the Form Flow Easily," we discuss why users make mistakes, how to help them overcome mistakes, and how to guide them through the form as a whole.

Chapter 7, "Taking Care of the Details," is about where to put the labels and how to indicate required fields, for example. This starts us on the appearance of forms.

Chapter 8, "Making a Form Look Easy," is about making your form look attractive, organized, and easy to navigate: the appearance layer.

Although many forms get issued without any testing, it's much, much better if you can try out your form before it starts doing any damage. In Chapter 9, "Testing (The Best Bit)," we explain why we love usability testing and how we go about testing forms.

Part 1
Relationship

Persuading People to Answer

1

If you understand people, you design better forms

When your form asks your user a question, you want an answer—a piece of information that the user has and you do not. This represents an investment, even if it is only a tiny one, by the user in the relationship with your organization.

The quality of the information that you can collect depends on the quality of the relationship at the moment when you ask the question.

In this chapter, we start with how people react to forms—how their relationship with the organization influences their reactions.

Then we explain how a theory from questionnaire design, "Social Exchange Theory," shows that we need to establish trust, offer rewards, and make forms easier to encourage people to answer.

And then the really crucial point: understanding your users. What makes them feel like trusting you? What reward do they want? What do they think of your organization?

How people react to forms

Let's look over the shoulder of two people as they work through a small form. This one is from the Open University.

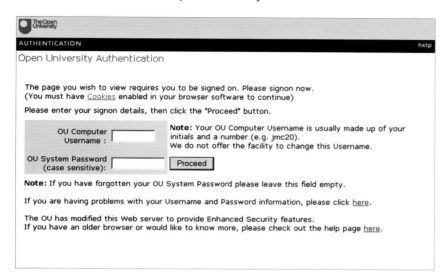

We'll start with Mike. He's retired from a job where he never used computers, and he's only recently got one. He's just joined the University, and he's signing on for the first time. He really wants to get this right.

When Mike sees the form, he's a bit worried. He glances first at the fields to type into, but he sees that there's a lot of text and he feels that he should read all of it.

He reads "You must have Cookies enabled in your browser software to continue" and thinks "Well, I haven't changed anything on this computer since I got it, so I'll have to hope that it's OK."

Then he gets to "case sensitive" and thinks "Eh? Not sure what that means. I'm going to have to hope it's OK again."

Despite his negative reaction, Mike really wants to sign up, so he persists.

Mike is a classic reader. He reads everything and will persist through the form until he succeeds with it.

Mike's interaction with the form is shown on the next page.

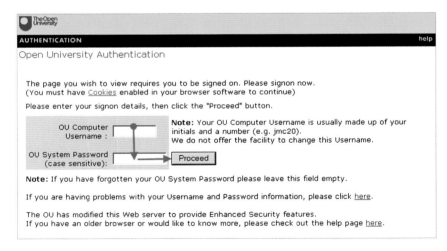

One interaction pattern with a form: glance at the boxes and then read it.

Rita is also a student at the Open University, but she is a year into her studies. She's younger and has used computers for years. She uses this form at least once a day. She hasn't read the text for months. Her usage pattern is like this:

- Look for the box to type into;
- Type;
- Look for the next box;
- Type;
- Look for the button. Done!

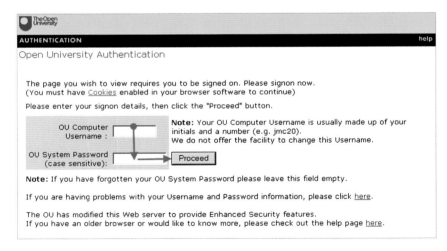

Another interaction pattern with a form: find the boxes, type, done.

To Rita, the form really looks like this; the area in focus is very small.

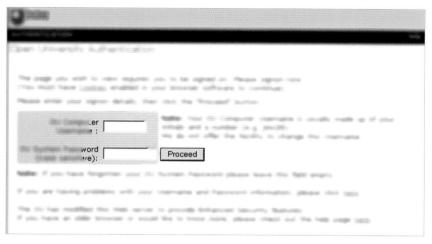

That Open University form is a few years old. Here's the new, redesigned version:

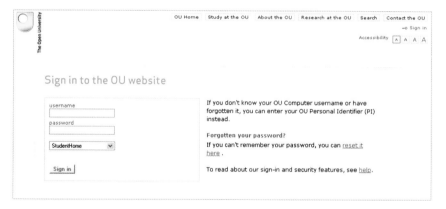

Readers, rushers, and refusers

Our first user, Mike, overcame his initial discomfort with the form and reacted by reading it. His desire to continue the relationship won.

Our second user, Rita, knows this form well enough to rush through it.

Other users might simply have nothing to do with the form. Perhaps being asked to sign in is off-putting, or more effort than it's worth.

Users of forms can be:

Readers	These users carefully read the form.
Rushers	These users rush in and begin completing fields, reading only when they think it is necessary.
Refusers	These users won't have anything to do with the form.

Most of us have forms that we rush, forms that we read, and forms that we refuse. For example, a taxation form with penalties for supplying incorrect information generally gets closer attention than the "yes, send me the e-newsletter" form in the margin of an interesting website. And a user encountering a website registration form might have any of these three reactions; it all depends on the value the user puts on continuing to use that website.

Think back to the last time you signed for a parcel. Did you rush, read, or refuse when you were given the receipt to sign?

Pick the right moment to ask a question

Asking for information at the wrong time can alienate a user. The same question put at the right moment can be entirely acceptable.

Think about buying a car. You're just browsing, getting a sense of what is available. A salesperson comes along and starts to ask you how you'll pay. Would you answer? Or would you think, "If that person doesn't stop annoying me, then I'm out to here"?

Now think about the point where you've told the salesperson which car you want to buy. Now it's appropriate to start negotiating about payment. It would be quite odd if the salesperson did NOT do so.

Is your form asking its questions at the right moment in the relationship?

Relationship varies question by question

The relationship can change from question to question. We sometimes see people work their way quite happily through most of a form, only to become annoyed or frustrated by one poorly placed or ill-considered question.

To help you in thinking about how relationship issues work, we've included an example. We'll listen in as a user talks through the form.

"I've heard about this web information sharing service from a colleague. Apparently, there's a free trial, so I plan to visit the website and sign up for the trial. I don't really know what it is, but I'm hoping that I'll learn through the trial.

"OK, I'll type in the URL. I'm looking for www.e-vis.com"

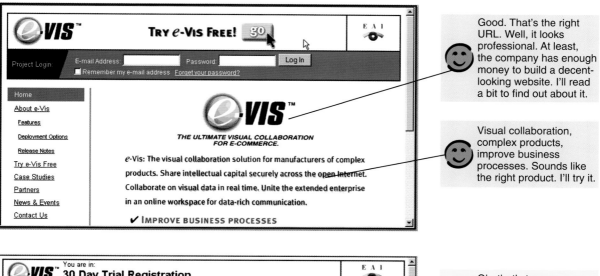

Good. That's the right URL. Well, it looks professional. At least, the company has enough money to build a decent-looking website. I'll read a bit to find out about it.

Visual collaboration, complex products, improve business processes. Sounds like the right product. I'll try it.

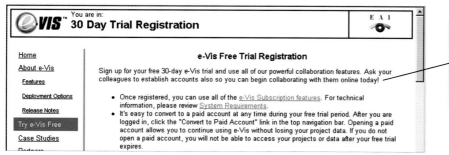

Oh, that's too many words. I've already decided to sign up, so I'll skip that. I've got to fill in the form. Where is it? Looks like I'll have to scroll.

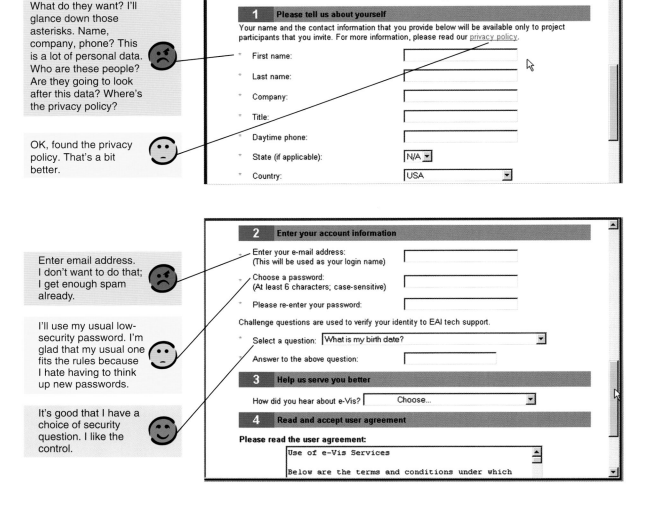

And so it continues until the end of the form. A bit up, a bit down.

Of course, not all users will react in the same way that our user did, and they will rarely be as explicit as our user in analyzing their views. But if that relationship deteriorates too far, users bail out or start entering anything at all, merely to get to the end of the form.

Three rules that influence response rates

When thinking about how to persuade people to answer our questions, we aim to follow three rules that we've derived from Social Exchange Theory. The key idea behind Social Exchange Theory is that people will answer questions if they feel good about it.

Social Exchange Theory comes from our favorite book on questionnaire design: Dillman, 2000.

Rule 1: Establish trust.	People are more likely to respond to a question if they trust the organization that asks it and agree with the purpose for which the information will be used. If they don't trust you, they'll either drop out of the form or lie to you.
Rule 2: Reduce social costs.	Social costs are bad feelings, like being made to feel inferior or being put at a disadvantage.
Rule 3: Increase rewards.	People are more likely to respond if they perceive that they will get some reward by doing so.

An immediate, small reward can be more effective than a delayed, bigger reward.

For example, in 1992, Jeannine M. James and Richard Bolstein reported on an experiment where they tested the effect of monetary incentives on a mail survey of owners of small construction subcontracting companies. They compared the effect of sending $1 in cash with the survey, compared to an offer of a guaranteed $50 check to be sent once the questionnaire was returned.

James and Bolstein (1992)

- The $1 sent with the survey significantly increased the response rate.
- The promise of $50 did not result in a significantly higher response rate than the control group who got nothing.

A small gift set up a social exchange that meant a significant proportion of respondents felt under an obligation to the questionnaire. The immediate dollar bill shows trust in the respondent, whereas the deferred reward means that the respondent had to trust the questionnaire provider.

If 1992 seems like a long time ago, check out this research. In 2005, Rob Burnside, Glenys Bishop, and Tenniel Guiver of the Australian Bureau of Statistics found that including the web address of a free (and relevant) report with a survey going to small businesses significantly increased the response rate. A small reward that showed trust.

Burnside, Bishop, and Tenniel (2005)

Rule 1: Establish trust

Our guidelines on trustworthiness for forms are developed from the Stanford guidelines (Fogg, 2002) on web credibility. http://www.webcredibility.org/guidelines/

Much of the trustworthiness of a form is inherited from the organization that issues it and from the website that contains it. The form itself can reinforce that credibility by following these guidelines—or undermine it by failing to do so.

To increase trust

1. Show that the form is published by a real organization.
2. Make it easy to contact the organization that publishes the form.
3. Ensure that the form has a clear purpose.
4. Make sure that the form looks as if it has been designed by a professional.
5. Keep advertising away from the form.
6. Check that the form works correctly: no defects, no typographical errors.

Rule 2: Reduce social costs

"Social costs" are anything that makes users feel bad or look bad to others. Forms can create social costs by asking intrusive or difficult questions, throwing away users' work if they make a mistake, or expecting an excessive effort relative to the users' goals.

To reduce social cost

1. Ask for answers; don't demand them.
2. Keep the form short and easy.
3. Help users to feel in control of the form by giving them a progress indicator or summary menu.
4. Minimize requests for sensitive or personal information.
5. Design questions that users can answer.
6. Use error messages that respect the effort the user is making.
7. If the user does make a mistake, preserve as much of that user's work as possible. Keep retyping to the minimum necessary to correct the problem.

Rule 3: Increase rewards

What reward does your user get from filling in your form? Is it access to your information, or are you providing a service? Or is it a no-incentive questionnaire, where the "reward" consists of simply getting a good feeling about helping you out?

Suppose you're browsing around the website of some high-profile consumer brand; let's say Coca-Cola.

Would you give this site your email address if asked for it?

Would you give your email address if the company promised to send you a voucher you could exchange for a can of Coke? a crate of Coke? a crate of Coca-Cola branded beverage of your choice?

A small reward: give them a form when they want one

One simple reward that you can arrange is to give people a form *when they want one*. Here's a comparison: renewing your vehicle's registration in Virginia compared to the same process in another nearby state. We started at the home page for the Department of Transportation in each state. Let's look at Virginia:

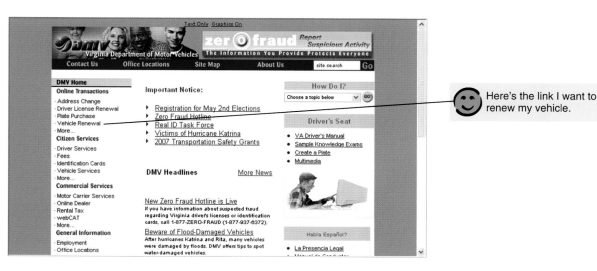

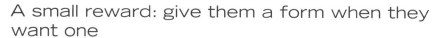

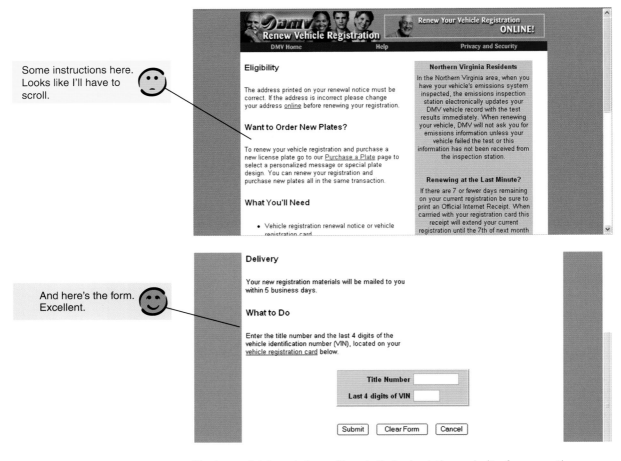

Some instructions here. Looks like I'll have to scroll.

And here's the form. Excellent.

That was fairly painless. Now let's look at the website from another nearby state.

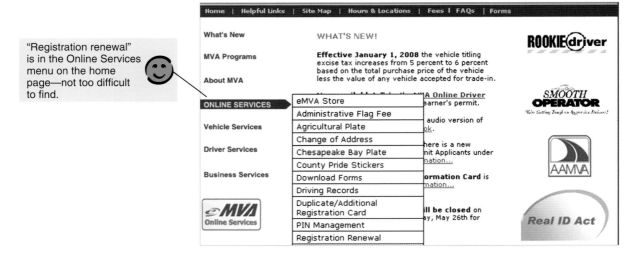

"Registration renewal" is in the Online Services menu on the home page—not too difficult to find.

What's New

MVA Programs
About MVA
ONLINE SERVICES
Administrative Flag Fees
Background Scene Plates
Change of Address
County Pride Stickers
Download Forms
Driving Records
Duplicate Registration Card
eMVA Store Home
PIN Management
Registration Renewal
Replacement Title
Temporary Registration
Transaction Status Check
VEIP Extension

Vehicle Services
Driver Services
Business Services

██████'s Online Vehicle Registration Renewal

Welcome to e-MVA! In today's fast-paced world, the MVA understands the need to make our services more convenient for you. We aim to simplify your life, and now you can renew your vehicle registration right over the Internet. Here's how:

- **Follow the simple instructions.**

- **You may renew up to 10 vehicles per purchase**
  - If you wish to renew more than 10 vehicles please complete this purchase before attempting to begin another

- **You will also need:**
  - The vehicle title number
  - The license plate number
  - A Visa, MasterCard or check
    (money orders & travelers checks not accepted)

- **Temporary Registration**
  Upon completing a registration renewal transaction, you will have the **option** to print a Temporary Registration. This document will enable you to operate your vehicle until your registration card and sticker arrive by mail within 10 days. A TEMPORARY REGISTRATION is not transferable and may not be used on a vehicle other than the one to which it was issued.

Renew Your Vehicle

 Now I need to read some instructions and click Renew Your Vehicle.

What's New

MVA Programs
About MVA
ONLINE SERVICES
Administrative Flag Fees
Background Scene Plates
Change of Address
County Pride Stickers
Download Forms
Driving Records
Duplicate Registration Card
eMVA Store Home
PIN Management
Registration Renewal
Replacement Title
Temporary Registration

Registration Renewal

If you wish to renew your registration only please click on Registration Renewal to continue.

If your vehicle is eligible and you wish to order a Background Scene Plate, please choose the option below. This will require you to renew your registration at the same time that you are ordering your plate.

REGISTRATION RENEWAL   BACKGROUND SCENE

 I've already clicked twice for renewal, and I have to do it again! This is getting annoying.

What's New

MVA Programs
About MVA
ONLINE SERVICES
Administrative Flag Fees
Background Scene Plates
Change of Address
County Pride Stickers
Download Forms
Driving Records
Duplicate Registration Card
eMVA Store Home
PIN Management
Registration Renewal
Replacement Title

Important Information!

Who Can Use the eMVA On-Line Registration Renewal Service?

- Most people with a passenger vehicle, motorcycle, trailer or truck under 26,000 lbs. can use this service.
- To renew your registration, your tags must expire within the next two months, or have already expired.
- If you have outstanding parking tickets, insurance violations, etc., you cannot use this service and you will have to visit one of our MVA Full Service Offices.

 Now I have to scroll through even more instructions. Where IS this form?

Users want to get the job finished quickly. Don't make them wander around your website looking for the form.

How long can your form be?

We're often asked "How long can a form be?"

The form is the right length if these factors are in balance:

- There is a basis of trust: the user trusts the organization enough to put in some effort.
- The user perceives that there is sufficient reward for completing the form.
- The effort (mental effort, number of questions, time to complete the form) is appropriate.

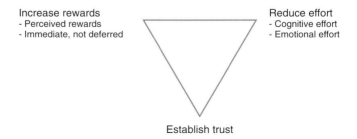

Increase rewards
- Perceived rewards
- Immediate, not deferred

Reduce effort
- Cognitive effort
- Emotional effort

Establish trust

So the form needs to be long enough to ask the relevant questions, to be short enough to minimize the user's effort, and to ask questions that are appropriate within the context of the overall relationship.

Who will answer your questions?

To understand whether we're offering the right reward to our users, we have to think about them. Who are they? What do they want to achieve with the form?

Understanding your users is often called "user profiling" or "user needs analysis."

The effort involved in compiling descriptions of your users depends on how well you know them. If, for example, you're designing a form to be used within your own organization, then it will be easier. Visit them, talk to them, find out why they need to fill in the form, determine how much computer experience they have.

Design for physical abilities and differences

In many countries, you are likely to be under a legal obligation to ensure that people with disabilities have equal access to your form. You do not necessarily have to provide exactly the same route for people with disabilities as for other people, but it will be a lot easier to maintain your forms if you have one form that works for people whether or not they have disabilities.

Statistics for disabilities vary greatly worldwide. This seems to be mostly due to differences in the definition of the term *disability* and therefore in the wording of questions about disability in censuses. However, the general view in the developed world is that around 10% of the population has some sort of disability. The most crucial problems for us as forms designers are:

The United Nations publishes statistics on disability taken from census records at http://unstats. un.org/unsd/demographic/ sconcerns/disability/

- Vision problems that make it hard for people to read;
- Motor control problems that make it hard for people to use the mouse to choose entries or to use the keyboard to type;
- Cognitive problems that make it hard for people to understand the form.

Find out about your users by asking them

If your users are external to your organization, finding out about them is a bit more difficult. But it's really worth the effort to get out there and meet them. If the information they provide is something they'd fill in as part of their home or leisure activities, then aim to visit some of them at home. If it's work-related, go to their workplace.

We think the best book on how to plan and learn from visits to users is still the one by Hackos and Redish (1998).

If talking to your users isn't practical, then try some of the other sources listed here. Aim to make sure you're designing for real people rather than "just anyone."

Adapted from Quesenbery, 2006.

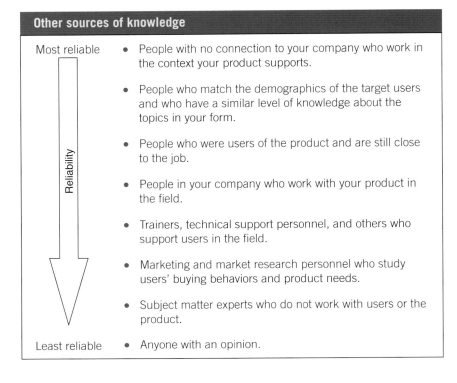

Other sources of knowledge

Most reliable

Reliability

- People with no connection to your company who work in the context your product supports.
- People who match the demographics of the target users and who have a similar level of knowledge about the topics in your form.
- People who were users of the product and are still close to the job.
- People in your company who work with your product in the field.
- Trainers, technical support personnel, and others who support users in the field.
- Marketing and market research personnel who study users' buying behaviors and product needs.
- Subject matter experts who do not work with users or the product.

Least reliable
- Anyone with an opinion.

Find out how users perceive the form

It's really important to understand users' perceptions **before** they see the form. Ask them these questions.

Relationship questions to ask your users (before they fill in your form)

1. What are you trying to achieve by filling in this form? Is it a step in an overall process, or will you be finished once you've finished the form?
2. What information are you expecting to provide?
3. Would it worry you if you had to give personal information on this form?
4. Do you expect to answer questions on the form from what's in your head? Or do you expect to have to ask other people or to look things up?
5. How long are you expecting to take to fill in this form? How much time can you spare?
6. What else is happening when you fill in this form? For example, do you get interrupted? Is it quiet or noisy?

There's more about testing your forms with users in Chapter 9.

After you have their answers to these relationship questions, then get them to fill out the form. Watch carefully: it's fascinating to see users' field-by-field reactions to forms.

Do you know enough about your users?

If you're thinking "I know my users; I don't need to hassle them," that's fine. Just look back over our list of questions in the preceding section and see how confident you are when you try to answer them on behalf of your users. Be honest!

If you're thinking "My users could be anyone; it's the web," that's true. But there is a difference between who your users *could* be and who they are *likely* to be.

We find that it's often helpful to choose two key, contrasting groups of users to help us think through the users we're designing for. Then we think about the relationship questions.

Even if you're designing a form that is used solely within your own organization, it's worth trying to find contrasting groups of users. Do some people use it constantly, others only occasionally? Are some people in a quiet office, others out on the road?

Here's an example: We've looked at two groups of users for the hotel booking site of a well-known hotel chain:

- busy professionals who are on a routine trip;
- retired leisure travelers who are planning the "trip of a lifetime."

Relationship questions	User group: busy professionals	User group: retired leisure
1. What are you trying to achieve by filling in this form? Is it a step in an overall process, or will you be finished once you've finished the form?	I need somewhere to lay my head on my next business trip. When I've done this form, I'm finished.	It's a step in getting my trip planned.
2. What information are you expecting to provide?	I expect to fill in the dates I want, a couple of personal details, and the method of payment. That's it.	Definitely our arrival and departure dates. And we want to choose a sightseeing tour. And it's our wedding anniversary. Will there be space to tell them about that?
3. Would it worry you if you had to give personal information on this form?	Nope, but it's a bit annoying because I often stay with this chain, and why don't they remember me?	No, I'm expecting to tell them all about our special requests.
4. Do you expect to answer questions on the form from just what's in your head, or are you expecting to have to ask other people or look things up?	May have to check my itinerary to get the right dates, but I'd be very surprised if I had to ask someone else.	We'll have to check everything, and we'll probably print a copy to think about. Might even talk it through with someone before we commit.
5. How long are you expecting to take to fill in this form? How much time can you spare?	Want to be done within a minute or two.	Happy to spend up to half-an-hour checking that everything is just right.
6. What else is happening when you fill in this form? For example, do you get interrupted? Is it quiet or noisy?	Telephone is ringing, dealing with email, last-minute discussion with colleagues.	A quiet moment at home.

Now think about designing the hotel booking form. Will one form meet both sets of needs? Probably, but we're going to have to think carefully about how to provide a speedy, simple path through it for our business professional while also giving the extra information and options that our retired leisure travelers require.

Make your facts about users into pictures of real people by creating personas

It's much easier to make useful design decisions and understand what you're trying to achieve if you create personas.

Definition

A *persona* is a description of a made-up person who reflects the characteristics of your target users.

The more realistic the personas, the easier it is to envisage whether or not we are serving them adequately in the design.

An example of using personas

We worked with the Institute of Chartered Accountants in England and Wales on the design of a form that asks Chartered Accountants a few complex questions about the ownership and conduct of their business, plus many routine questions such as the address of the business. The Chartered Accountants have to complete this form every year as a condition of continuing their practice.

We helped the designers to create these personas:

- Leonard, the Chartered Accountant, is in his 40s. He started in practice on his own 10 years ago. He has the professional qualifications and the legal responsibility for the quality of the work his firm does and the conduct of the business.
- Marge is a 50-something office administrator/bookkeeper. She runs the commercial side of the firm but is not involved in the technical work.
- Gerald, 27, Leonard's assistant, helps with the technical work of the firm and is attending evening classes because he eventually hopes to get professional qualifications.

As the designers thought about the personas, they realized that although Leonard had the legal responsibility and would have to answer the complex questions, he would probably want to delegate the process of answering the routine questions to Gerald or Marge.

This conclusion showed that the designers needed to create two types of logon: one that would allow a user to fill in questions but not to sign the final form and another that would additionally allow the user to sign the form. They also needed to design the form so that it could be saved without being signed.

Try creating a persona and be sure to try making up the "story" that gives some background as to why the persona is working with your form.

Does this seem too abstract? Then try explaining the bare facts about the persona to a couple of colleagues and then tell them the story. We predict that the story conveys the reality of the user better than the bare facts.

Note: If you already have personas for your website, then why not use the same ones for your forms design?

Summary

Asking for data from people requires a commitment from them, even if it is tiny. To ensure that you get honest and timely data from your users, make sure that you:

- Pick the right moment to ask a question;
- Think about who will use the form and his or her relationship with the organization;
- Understand the user's goals associated with the form;
- Ensure that the reward the user gets from filling in the form is in balance with the amount of effort required to complete it.

We're often asked about how to design registration forms. Organizations love them: "We'll justify/protect/market/leverage this content by asking people to register for it."

Now the sad thing about registration forms is that users hate them. Stick a form in front of them and they leave your site, they lie, or if they are really web-savvy they use a privacy protection service such as Bugmenot (www.bugmenot.com).

Bugmenot is a privacy protection service. We don't recommend it: we're just warning you that it exists.

In the last chapter, we pointed out that it's a bad idea to ask a question at the wrong moment. And that's exactly what registration forms do: ask questions before the user is ready to answer.

So the first line of argument is to try to avoid asking users to register at all. But we know that this is an unrealistic position, because there will always be commercial or political pressures for registration. So how can we limit the damage and make the registration process as easy as possible?

Explain why you're asking

If you shove the questions at the users without any justification, they won't be happy. Offer a reward: put in a very short sentence that says why you are asking them to register.

Offer something that users want

The reward that you offer for registering must be something that benefits the user—not something that benefits your organization.

One way of persuading users to register is to offer them some way of sampling the reward they'll get from registering. You could give them the top couple of paragraphs of an article, a couple of screen-shots from a demo, or a sample of the newsletter they're subscribing to.

Offering "something for nothing" helps to establish trust.

The fewer questions, the better

Your users are busy people and you're interrupting them. Be polite: keep the interruptions to a minimum.

Can you restrict your registration form to a single question? Great, go for it.

For example, if all you really need to do is assure yourself that you are dealing with adults for legal reasons, then just ask the single question: "Are you over 18?".

Avoid invasive questions

It's even more important to be careful about asking invasive questions, such as personal data.

Users don't like giving out their personal data: asking them for it creates a social cost and reduces your response rate.

And in most countries, there are laws about how you handle personal data. Ask someone's name and you're into the world of privacy policies ... a whole topic in itself.

Ask once only

If you offer an appropriate reward and keep to a small number of questions that appear to be relevant to the purpose of your form then users will register.

But don't overdo it. They have registered once: don't surprise them by asking them to register again.

If the first level of registration only offers a small part of the rewards of the site then that's fine. But be honest about what they'll get access to—and what they won't get access to.

So our final rule is: don't surprise people with multiple levels of registration.

An example of a registration form

We're often asked for a good example of a form. The problem is that there is no example that is universally good. Here's one that we like (with some reservations).

People who are interested in the Sun Developer Network are likely to be rather tech-savvy and we don't have any concerns about technical issues like what it means to register.

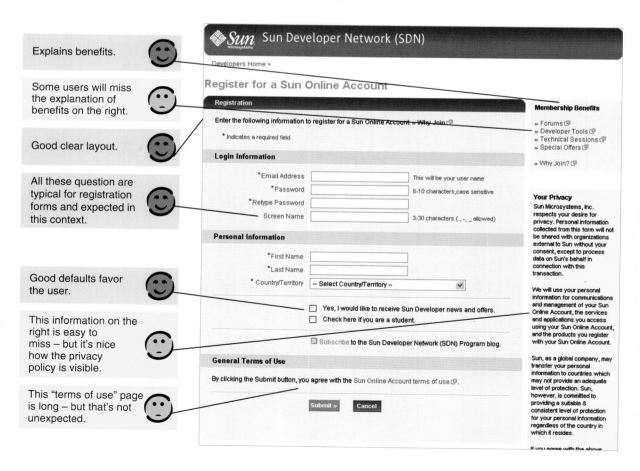

Asking for the Right Information

Find out why you need the information

Forms have a tendency to gather information long after its usefulness has ceased. Here are a couple of examples:

- Someone in the warehouse used to rely on a stock code to pick the item from the shelf, but the new warehousing system doesn't use stock codes.

- Someone in marketing ran a specific analysis about the effectiveness of different types of advertising and then made a decision, moved onto another project, and forgot to tell you that it's no longer interesting.

Conversely, if you ask users to give you some information, then they expect that you will use it.

For example, we were testing a form that allowed users to order a printed brochure. It asked for the obvious information (name and address) but also asked for email address. Users were convinced that they would be notified by email when the brochure was sent out—even though there was nothing on the form to tell them that, and the organization had no plans to use the email address in this way. The simple solution: stop asking for email addresses.

Every piece of information you ask for puts a burden on your user and creates a burden on your organization to do something with it. You want to be sure that the effort is justified.

So before you think about how you will collect the information, you need to find out how your organization will use the information you collect.

Ask your stakeholders

Anyone who has an interest in your form is a stakeholder. For example:

- whoever is paying for it;
- your manager and other co-workers developing the form;
- departments that will use the information that you gather;
- departments that have an interest in the impact on your users or customers, such as marketing or customer service;
- probably other people, sometimes outside the organization.

We try to talk to as many of these people as we can. What do they think the purpose of the form is—from the organization's point of view? What do they see as "success" for this form? Do they see any barriers to that success?

Typically, we run into one of these two problems:

1. No one is interested. The organization hasn't thought about how it will use the information and doesn't want to.

   If this happens to you, you may find that designing the form is easy at first because there is no interference, but becomes difficult later, when people suddenly start to think about what you're proposing.

   Solution: Record your decisions and make sure you have offered formal and informal opportunities to stakeholders to get involved.

2. Everyone is far too interested. Senior managers arrive at meetings. There are many opinions, all fervently held and often contradictory.

   If this happens to you, you'll find that it's tough going at first. Keep working at getting consensus, and you'll have a much easier ride later.

   Solution: Concentrate on users and do plenty of testing (see Chapter 9). Try to make sure that the decisions are based on data rather than opinions.

Using personas to bring out differences and establish consensus

Faced with a set of stakeholders and not sure how to get them involved in the decisions about your form?

We often start the process by having a "personas workshop."

1. Ask your stakeholders to work in pairs.
2. Get each pair to write a persona for the typical user of your form. (You can use the relationship questions in Chapter 1 to prompt them.)
3. Then get the pairs to tell everyone else about their particular persona.

During the discussion, we usually find that stakeholders realize that they don't know the answers to some of the relationship questions. For example, they may not know where the users find some of the answers. This often helps us to get agreement for activities aimed at establishing the facts about users.

The main outcome from the discussion is usually one of these:

- Everyone's personas are somewhat similar. This is good because it shows that there is a consensus about who is using your form. One caution: Check that the typical user really is typical and ask yourself whether you need to find out about other user groups.

- The personas are rather disparate. This is also good because it shows that you are thinking about many different users and their needs. We try to build consensus around no more than five main user groups.

Either way, it's a good idea to compare these personas with the ones you thought about in Chapter 1. Taking this action helps you, and your stakeholders, to concentrate on the users you are designing for.

Ask the people who work with the information

We find that it is crucial to identify the specific individual who really uses each answer. Don't settle for "the marketing department needs it" or "they use it in the human resources department" or "customer services looks at that." Go out and hunt down a real person or two who can show you exactly what they do with the information.

Our rule of thumb for whether we've found the right people is to ask "What do you do if you get the wrong answer or no answer to that question?" If they seem unsure, maybe you need to ask someone else.

Another good way to explore how the information is really used is to employ a "critical incident technique." Get them to talk you through a specific example. We ask them to show us how they dealt with something easy, a typical example, and a difficult one. Ask for the "tips and tricks" that they use to get through a real day (as opposed to the "official" way that it's supposed to be done). If we possibly can, we like to sit one-on-one at each individual's desk or cubicle: it's easier to tell a single interviewer about your private way of working than to announce it to a whole roomful of people.

There is a short explanation of critical incident technique at www.ul.ie/~infopolis/methods/incident.html.

Use a question protocol to think about how information is used

If your form is complicated or you think that there is any risk of disagreements between different departments about what you need to know, then you need a question protocol.

A *question protocol* is a list of:

Definition

- every question you ask;
- the people who use the answer for each question within your organization;
- what they use it for;
- whether the answer is required or optional.

If the answer is required, the question protocol determines what will happen if the user enters "any old thing" in order to get through the form.

Question protocols are tedious to compile but essential if you need to arbitrate between conflicting views of the information you need.

When we create question protocols, it usually becomes obvious that we're not sure about some of the information. So then we set up a few meetings with the different departments to wring the answers out of them.

Check whether your organization already holds the information

Now that you know what information you need, the next step is to think about where it has to come from and whether you even need to ask your users about it.

Use information that already exists in your organization

Sometimes you can use information that already exists (either with or without having the users check it). Other times you have to ask the users for the information.

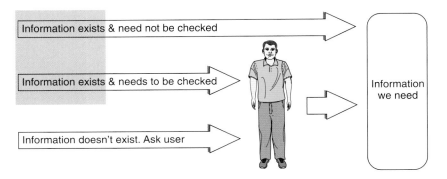

Some of the information you hold can be, or must be, used without asking the users anything. For example:

- credit rating from a credit checking agency;
- whether users are eligible for special loyalty discounts based on previous buying history.

These information items do not appear on the form but instead are collected from a database somewhere. For example, in the UK and New Zealand, many people with jobs never have to do a tax return. Instead, the tax authorities use their databases of information collected from the employers. The tax deduction system works so that employees pay the right amount of tax: no refunds are due, nothing extra to pay, and no need to check with the taxpayer.

(Incidentally, while this approach seems fine in New Zealand and the UK, people in the USA sometimes find it smacks of "Big Brother." Attitudes differ within cultures, and you need to be aware of them when designing.)

Often you need to allow the users to check the information that you already hold. For example:

- credit card to use (generally displayed with some digits obscured);
- shipping address.

This information is gathered from a database and prepopulates part of the form. All the users need to do is check that the information is correct or change it as necessary.

Let's look at some of the information on this page from Amazon.com.

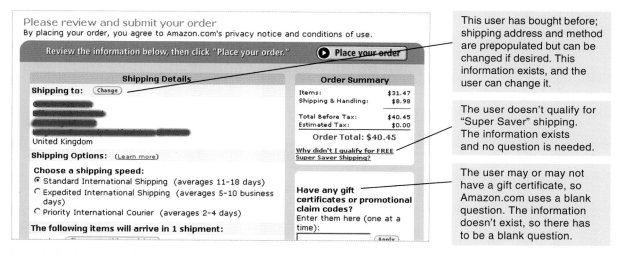

This user has bought before; shipping address and method are prepopulated but can be changed if desired. This information exists, and the user can change it.

The user doesn't qualify for "Super Saver" shipping. The information exists and no question is needed.

The user may or may not have a gift certificate, so Amazon.com uses a blank question. The information doesn't exist, so there has to be a blank question.

Avoid duplication

Despite the advantages to users of not having to answer questions, we find that organizations often resist using information that they already have. Why? Because the necessary database isn't easily available, and it seems easier to ask users for extra answers than to tackle the technical problems of extracting the data.

We can't decide for you whether the short-term technical pain is worth it for the longer-term user benefit, but we'd like to throw in one other argument: the need to avoid duplication.

Think about asking for names and addresses. Users often have small variations in the way they enter them. For example:

Name:	Jane P. Smith	Mrs J. P. Smith
Address:	1 Any St. Apartment 3, This Town AR 01337	1 Any Street, Apt 3, This Town, Arkansas 01337

This example shows the same person at the same address, but some systems would fail to detect that. The result is a user with two records, with all the associated problems this may cause.

Find out what others ask for

When we were thinking about users, we recommended that you find out what they are expecting to do both in terms of what you are asking and also of what similar organizations or competitors ask.

If your users feel that your form asks for everything that is necessary and is shorter than your competitors' form, then your form will be more successful.

You probably won't be able to get your competitors to tell you how they use the information that they gather, but it's usually rather easy to find out what they ask for.

If you're asking for more information than your competitors do, you need to consider whether your request is justified by something you do differently (and, we hope, better).

What to do if you don't have competitors

If you're thinking "we don't have competitors," then think about who is competing for your users' time and information:

- Look for the websites that serve these audiences for other purposes. For example, if you are a government department, then you could look at government gateways such as www.usa.gov, www.australia.gov.au, or www.direct.gov.uk.
- Look at how other jurisdictions tackle the same problem. Is there a similar organization in another district or country?
- Ask some users what other forms they use from day to day and whether they think that any of them are comparable to the form that they complete for you.

An example of looking at competitors

We were helping a leading business school to design their application form. We knew that students would consider both this school and at least one other. So we looked at:

- the school's own form;
- the leading regional competitor;
- a well-known school outside the region.

Summary: Ask for information that you need

Find out why you're asking your users for information, what you're going to do with it, and when you need it:

- Asking for information that you don't need is bad.

- Check with stakeholders to see what information is really needed.

- Users will assume that you will actually use the information you request, so make sure you do use it in a sensible way.

- Find out what your competitors and similar organizations are doing.

Case Study

A conference booking form: A sample question protocol

We've described a question protocol as a list of every question you want to ask, with associated information about why you're asking it and what you'll do with the information.

Here's an example showing how a question protocol worked in practice. We were working on a conference booking form in the UK.

The typical users were:

- individuals who wanted to attend the conference themselves;
- administrative staff who were booking places at the conference on behalf of a group of individuals from their organization.

It was a popular conference, with reasonable rates and limited places. The users were happy to book their places, and the conference appealed to people who were comfortable with the Internet and with forms.

Before continuing, you might like to make a note of the questions you'd expect to answer on a conference booking form.

It was a small, simple organization, and we had only a few stakeholders:

- Marketing: responsible for advertising the conference and public relations;
- Presenters: responsible for teaching the tutorials that made up the conference;
- Conference office: responsible for all administration of the conference, including all payments apart from credit cards;
- Credit card company: a third-party credit card service that handled credit card payments.

Our questions, who needs the answer, and our notes are in the table opposite.

A question protocol for a conference registration form

Answer (Required fields in red with *)	Who needs it?	For what (our initial notes)?
Title	Conference office	Do we still need to ask for titles? We used to be more formal than we are now.
*Name	Conference office	Letter to confirm booking
Job title	Conference office Presenters	Why for conference office? Presenters need it for planning.
Organization	Conference office Marketing	Letter to confirm booking To check against list of target customers
*Address	Conference office	Letter to confirm booking
*Telephone number	Conference office	In case there are any difficulties with booking
Fax number	Conference office	Why? When did we last send a fax to a conference attendee?
Email	Conference office	In case there are any difficulties with booking
*Choice of tutorial	Conference office Presenters	Letter to confirm booking To check numbers for tutorial
*Method of payment: direct transfer, credit card, invoice to organization	Conference office	To collect payment by the method preferred by delegate
If user chooses to pay by credit card: Cardholder's Name Company Name (if corporate card) Credit card type Credit Card Number Expiry Date Security code Valid From Date (Diners Only) Cardholder's billing address	 Credit card company Credit card company Credit card company Credit card company Credit card company Credit card company Credit card company Conference office	 Required for authorization Required for authorization Required for authorization Required for authorization Required for authorization Required for authorization Required for authorization In case credit card company queries the payment

Do you agree with our choice of required fields?

Do you have any suggestions about why the conference office staff may want a delegate's title and fax number?

We took our question protocol to a meeting with the conference office manager.

She said:

"Title: We're writing to the attendees and in the UK it is regarded as rude if we don't use a title."

"Job title: You have to have that. In a big organization there are often several people with the same name and the job title is the only way to be sure that the confirmation letter gets to the right person."

"Fax: we might have to fax over details at the last minute, or fax a copy invoice if there's a problem with payment."

Do you agree with the conference office manager that title, job title, and fax number should all be on the form? Or would you make a different decision?

In the end, we decided to retain title and job title but to remove fax number. In our discussions with the conference manager, we learned that she always talked to the attendee before faxing something, and she always needed a fax number near the attendee at that moment which might be different from the usual fax number. So it was better to ask for the fax number at the point it was needed.

Our conference form example showing a question protocol is straightforward. We wish it were always this easy! Unfortunately, we find that getting agreement on the question protocol often reveals tensions between departments.

In our case, Marketing happened to want information that is also necessary for another purpose (that is, the organization an attendee works for). But what if they wanted a question like "Where did you hear about this conference," requiring a complicated drop-down list? If this were the case, the users would have to do more work. Is that work justified? That's when the discussions about the real value of the data compared to the user's work can start.

Part 2
Conversation

Making Questions Easy to Answer

Ask questions that support smooth conversation

During an ordinary conversation, if one person asks a question that the other one doesn't understand, then there are many opportunities to backtrack, to clarify meaning, and to correct misconceptions.

Your form is a sort of conversation between the user and your organization, but this conversation takes place remotely, without those opportunities for clarification.

In this chapter, we start by analyzing the process of answering a question because a disruption of any detail of that will undermine the conversation. Then we go on to think about how to make each part of that process as easy as we can.

The four steps in answering a question

Answering questions is something that we do so naturally that it's not at all obvious what is going on. Nor do we often have to analyze it.

Our steps are based on the ideas in Tourangeau, Rips, and Rasinski (2000) about answering questions in surveys.

We watched a lot of people filling in and talking about forms, complex and simple. We thought about how people answer questions in surveys. We found that there are four steps in answering a question on a form:

1. Understand the question.
2. Find an answer.
3. Judge whether the answer fits the question.
4. Put the answer on the form.

These steps may happen almost together, or they may take quite a while.

For example, do you have to log on to your organization's computer systems, or to a website you use frequently? If so, you'll probably answer the questions on the logon form almost instantaneously—doing all four steps together and barely noticing that you've answered.

At the other extreme, Mark Barratt of Text Matters (http://www.textmatters. com) worked on a complex form for a UK government agency. The users were very large industries. To complete the form correctly, they had to:

- understand new and complex monitoring procedures;
- find the answer by setting up their organization's procedure—in effect, by creating it from scratch;
- judge the answer by getting their lawyers to agree that their proposed answers met the government's legal requirements and accurately reflected the new procedures;
- put their answers on the form—that bit was relatively easy.

Overall, the average cost for filling in the form was around £350,000 (equivalent to US$700,000), and it took about two years to fill in.

Most forms fall somewhere in between these two extremes, but the steps in the process are much the same.

So let's look at how these different steps can cause problems for users.

Consider the responses of a user looking at a typical login form on an e-commerce site. These are not particularly tricky questions, but each of them does pose a minor problem—each in a different area of answering the question.

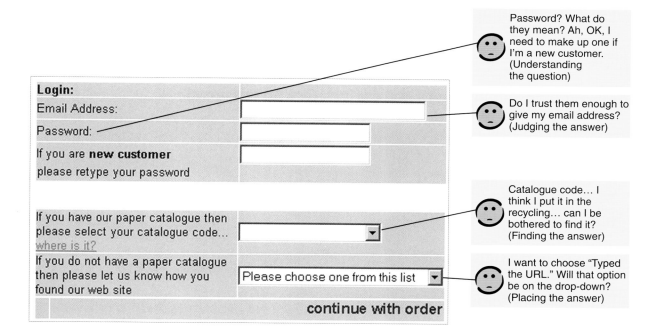

Of course, most people do not sit and agonize over each tiny element of answering a question. But they'll certainly notice if an element is out of place, and then they may become confused or annoyed.

Make the question easy to understand

We'll discuss legibility in Chapter 7.

Assuming that the text is legible, "understand the question" is about making sense of it, translating the form's question into something meaningful to the user.

Ask about familiar concepts using familiar words

We'll come back to using familiar words in familiar ways again in the next chapter, on writing instructions.

It's probably obvious that unfamiliar words or concepts are harder to understand. The challenge is that what is usual within your organization may be unusual from the point of view of the person filling in the form.

For example, the U.S. Department of Homeland Security has a form called "USCIS Form I-140 (Petition for Alien Worker)." This form has nothing to do with extraterrestrial life-forms: To Homeland Security, the word "alien" means anyone who is not a U.S. citizen.

Even something apparently straightforward can give the user a bit of a problem to decode. For example, the second question in the screenshot below uses the terms "In Care of Name" in one place and "C/O" in another. Perhaps these are obviously the same, but perhaps not—especially if the form has to be filled in by someone who speaks English as a second language.

"In Care of Name" becomes "C/O." Not totally clear.

In Care of Name: (1-26 letters) OPTIONAL	Do not type "C/O" in the field below. C/O

The instruction about "C/O" could be confusing.

Or, consider the pair of questions in the following screenshot. We found it straightforward to answer the first question because the concept of "presenting at a conference" is familiar. But what does "moderate the session" mean? Is the concept of "moderate" as a verb likely to be familiar to typical users of the form? If it is familiar, what does this conference mean by "moderate"? Will there be hordes of angry attendees who need restraint, or does this just mean "introduce yourself"?

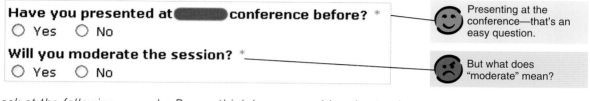

Presenting at the conference—that's an easy question.

But what does "moderate" mean?

Look at the following example. Do you think lawyers would understand this? Hairdressers? Computer programmers? Anyone you know who took up computing as a senior, perhaps your grandparents or parents?

This example is from the website of a well-known maker of movies for children. Maybe the kids would know (or find out and tell each other).

A weed is a plant that is growing in the wrong place. Jargon, like weeds, is a problem where it crops up in material that is intended for an audience that isn't familiar with it. Jargon is no problem at all if the users know what it means; then it becomes convenient shorthand for getting at mutually understood concepts.

The following screenshot is part of a form used inside an organization. At first glance, it looks incomprehensible because of the jargon. The users had no problems at all because they used the terms "Bucket Position" and "FTE" every day and therefore knew exactly how to fill in these boxes.

All the users of this form understood this jargon, no problem.

Ask one question at a time

It's probably obvious that questions are easier to answer if they ask about one thing at a time. But we often see two questions hidden in a single one. For example, suppose that you need to find out whether customers with an email address are willing to be contacted by email. It's tempting to write this question:

"If you have an email address, may we use it to contact you? Yes No".

The problem is that users have to unwrap this single question into its separate parts to be able to answer, and then there are more possibilities than answers:

- I have an email address; you can use it.   (Yes)
- I have an email address; you cannot use it.   (No)
- I don't have an email address.   (Yes or no?)

OK, so you wouldn't write the question that way. But these double questions can sneak up on you. For example, this form requires users to think about legal responsibility, residence, and whether the child was in their care. All at once.

These exclusions mean that users have to answer several questions at once.

Baby bonus
Dates you are not eligible for the baby bonus   [Help with this page]

Enter the start and end dates for any periods from 1/7/2006 to 25/4/2007 that you:

- did not have legal responsibility for and care of the child, and/or
- were not a resident of ▓▓▓▓, and/or
- were not the eligible person

Note: If the eligibility is being transferred to you, this screen is asking for the dates your spouse was not eligible.

If not applicable, click **Next**

Enter dates chronologically. Do **not** enter dates after the child's **fifth** birthday.

Some questions hide two questions in one. Look at the detail from this complaint form.

This is really two questions:
(1) "Do you know the name of the company that you are complaining about?"
(2) "If yes, please give the name here."

Name of Company You Are
Complaining About: [_____]

And the designers of the form clearly thought that there might be a problem because they included a checkbox as the next question.

These questions are definitely in the wron order.

Name of Company You Are
Complaining About:
Check If Company Name Is Unknown: ☐

Do you agree that the previous two-in-one question is a problem? Or maybe it doesn't matter because most users would see the follow-up checkbox?

We've often observed that users concentrate very narrowly on one question at a time. They don't look ahead, so they'd miss this follow-up question.

Turn negative questions into positive ones

Questions that include negatives can be harder to understand.

> ☑   may send you useful product and service information relevant to your booking, including offers and discounts for future bookings through us. We will however NOT provide your details to any third party, except in accordance with our terms and conditions, other than the train company you travel with. If you do not wish to receive this information simply untick the box.

Do not wish... untick the box... too many negatives. Confusing—especially after all those words before the question.

A typical double negative in marketing information. This one is from a train ticket business.

Double negatives, negative words, and negative phrasing all cause difficulties. For example, the sentence "Is the address we sent this form to wrong?" would be much better rewritten as "Did we send this form to the correct address?"

Hidden negatives can sneak into things that look positive at first glance. Look at the exclusions in the next screenshot. At a first reading, it seems positive: "if you can answer 'Yes'" is positive, and the exclusions are positive. But the overall intent is negative: if these apply to you, then you cannot apply online.

Can I apply online?

Unfortunately if you can answer "Yes" to any of the following questions we are **currently unable** to process your application online but your local branch will be happy to help:

☑ I'm an existing ██████████ Mortgage holder looking to simply **switch mortgage product**
☑ I'm an existing ██████████ Mortgage holder looking for a **Further Advance**
☑ I'm looking to buy or Remortgage a **Shared Ownership** property
☑ I'm looking to buy or Remortgage a **Right to Buy** property
☑ I'm looking to buy or Remortgage a **Shared Equity** property

These exclusions look positive but are negative.

Section from a mortgage application form.

Rather than use this hidden negative, we'd suggest turning it around so that it specifies the cases where users *can* apply online. For example,

"You can apply online if you are…"

Clarify meaning by careful grouping

You can solve problems of meaning by grouping your questions appropriately.

For example, we worked on the following conference registration form, where the organization emphasized the "online only" booking process. The user is expecting to provide contact information and pay the conference fee.

Name, company, email... that's all fine. 😊

But this is an online form; what's all this "mailing" stuff? ☹

And what's a key code? 😠

OK, credit card details—here's where they go. 😊

→ Your Full Name:

Company Name:

→ Your Job Title:

→ Email Address:

→ Telephone Number:

Fax Number:

→ Street Address:

→ City:

→ State/Province:

→ ZIP/Postal Code:

→ Country:

Mailstop/Room:

Key Code *:

*key code from label of any mailing you might have received advertising this event.
Leave blank if you don't have a code

→ Credit Card Number: `1111 2222 3333 4`

→ Name of Credit Card Owner: `xxx`

→ Expiration Date: `10` ▼ / `00` ▼

Because of their position in the conversation, the user assumes that the questions about mailing address are part of the general contact details—in other words that they will be used for contact details.

But, in fact, this information is not for contact purposes at all, but for credit card validation.

Rearranging the questions to place the address details with the credit card details fixed the problem. Incidentally, it also improves data quality: the draft in the example would have collected the contact address for the delegate, which might not be the same as the address for the credit card holder.

Get rid of decision points

Sometimes forms want users to decide between questions or parts of a question. At first glance, this next form looks just fine. It lets users look up the selling price of houses in the UK and offers users a choice between entering a postcode or a combination of street and town.

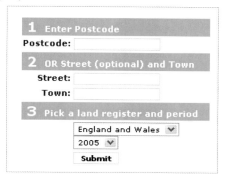

This form required a decision between questions 1 and 2.

But if we look at the typical form reading pattern, the problem with decisions becomes more obvious. When immersed in a form, users don't read the headings. Instead, they skip from field to field.

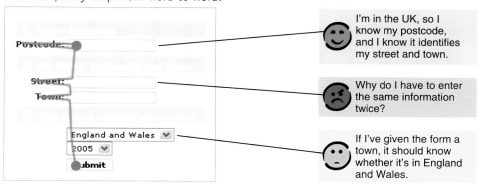

In a typical reading pattern, users will ignore the headings.

Decision points are tricky because they offer an implicit question that probably hasn't been identified: "Which option would you like to use?" And often users don't realize that there is an implicit question. The only solution that we've found for decision points is to get rid of them, and the current version of the same form does exactly that.

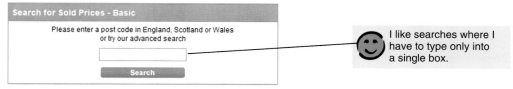

This form is not as pretty as the previous one, but it's easier to use.

Be aware of cultural biases

Cultural biases happen when the areas of experience of your users are different from what you expect.

For example, we recently traveled on a very busy train. A woman got on and was quite annoyed to find that her reserved "Quiet Zone" seat was in a section that was full, with no space left for her luggage. She was even more annoyed when she found that she wasn't allowed to use her cell phone in that coach.

I'll pick that; I don't like it when the train is too crowded.

How was I supposed to know that it means 'no cell phones'?

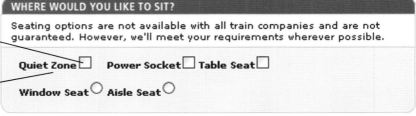

Booking options for seats on a train. "Quiet zone" means that cell phones are not allowed.

A more subtle type of bias appears when a form asks a question that explores an area of experience that is not usually part of the conversation. For example, think about putting your bank details into a form for setting up a payment. We'll assume that you trust the organization and that you are willing to divulge bank account details.

We tried this on one website.

Question about bank account.

Does the question about the bank account strike you as unusual, or is it familiar in the context of making a payment?

We found the question unusual. In the UK and Australia, most forms take the view that if you have given bank account details, then there is a mutual assumption that you are authorized to do so. There is no separate step asking you about it. So, although the wording of the question is reasonably clear, it does not conform to our experience; therefore, we found it a bit confusing.

These cultural conflicts can sneak up on you most unexpectedly. We find the best way to avoid them is by doing lots of usability testing with real target users.

Make it easy to find the answer

Once a user has understood the question, the next step is to find the answer.

Think of buying something from a website that you've visited for the first time. You've made your choice and clicked "Checkout" to finish the purchase. What questions do you expect to see? How do you expect to find the answers to those questions?

OK, so think about this scenario. It's Jane's mother's birthday. Mom lives in another city. It's summer and exceptionally hot, so Jane wants to make sure that someone will be at home to receive the flowers she has ordered. The following table describes some of the information that she needs and how she finds it:

Buying flowers for Mom		
Information Jane needs	**How she finds it**	**What we call this type of answer**
Name of purchaser	In her head	Slot-in
Method of payment	Gets the credit card out of her wallet	Gathered
Time of delivery	Makes a phone call to check when Mom will be home	Third-party
Message	Thinks for a couple of minutes to make up something appropriate	Created

This rather ordinary transaction demonstrates the four different ways that people find answers to questions.

Slot-in answers are in our heads

Slot-in answers are the ones we hold in our heads: everyday information, such as our own names and addresses.

Sometimes this information is almost automatic, stored in "muscle memory" in the fingers for typing. Sometimes it's completely automatic, if you have chosen to use one of the automatic form-fill programs such as Google AutoFill or Roboform.

http://toolbar.google.com
http://www.roboform.com/.

Gathered answers are found somewhere else

Gathered answers come from somewhere that the user can get to personally: on a card, in a desk drawer, on the computer, in a wallet, at the office. Occasionally, these answers are found by retrieving something from the user's more distant memories.

The level of difficulty of these answers depends on the importance to the user of the item he or she needs to find. Is it something like a credit card number that he or she will use most days? Or is it a reference number jotted down on a piece of paper months ago and forgotten meanwhile?

Gathering the answer isn't always easy.

Third-party answers come from someone else

To find a third-party answer, the user has to ask someone else. For example, we might know that a family member takes a medication for a specific condition but have to ask for the exact name of that medication.

The questions requiring this type of answer are not all that common on forms, but they can cause quite a bit of extra work for users. Or, there is a temptation to skip these questions or make up answers.

Created answers are made up on the spot

An answer is "created" if it isn't slot-in, gathered, or third-party. Sometimes created answers are choices that the user could not reasonably have made in advance. Other created answers require actual imagination.

Some "created" answers require only the tiniest, easiest amount of thought. "Are you planning to take a vacation next year?" usually requires a created answer, but is it a tricky one for you or is the answer quite straightforward?

"Shipping method" is often a created answer.

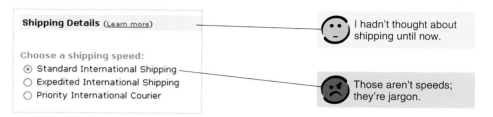

Shipping Details (Learn more)

Choose a shipping speed:
- ⦿ Standard International Shipping
- ○ Expedited International Shipping
- ○ Priority International Courier

I hadn't thought about shipping until now.

Those aren't speeds; they're jargon.

Mismatches in answering strategies create problems

All these answering strategies are just fine. The problems arise when you expect users to use one strategy, but in fact they use another.

For example, we bought a new printer and the registration form asked "How many pages do you print each month?" At first, this question seems to expect a slot-in answer. But the answer wasn't in our heads—not slot-in. It wasn't written down anywhere, nor was it something we could retrieve from distant areas of memory, so we couldn't gather it. No one in our office monitors printer usage, so we couldn't ask anyone else. The only strategy left was creating an answer. In other words, we guessed—and probably not very accurately. Quite easy for us, but was the answer any use to the printer company?

Market researchers are familiar with the need to be careful about asking people for opinions. If you force people to express an opinion, they are likely to create one just to get through your form. The problem is that opinions created on the spot are variable, as many opinion pollsters know to their cost.

Sometimes the mismatches can be rather subtle.

Suppose you want to travel as a tourist to Australia for the first time and you are not Australian. You have learned that you need a visa and that you can get one called an Electronic Travel Authority (ETA) *on the Web. What answering strategy would you expect to use for these questions?*

Type of ETA:
Are you outside Australia:
Passport Number:
Nationality:
Date of Birth:
Family Name:

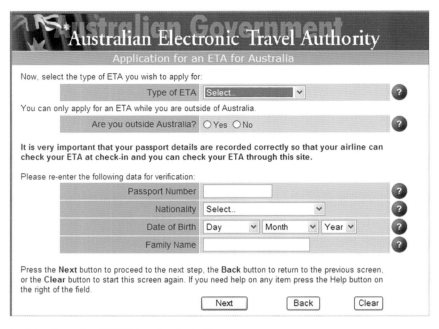

Applying for a visa ("ETA") to enter Australia.

If you have traveled to Australia recently, you may consider that all these answers are slot-in. Our view is:

Type of ETA	Gathered, third-party, or created
Are you outside Australia	Slot-in
Passport Number	Gathered (from the user's passport)
Nationality	Slot-in
Date of Birth	Slot-in
Family Name	Slot-in

"Type of ETA" is probably the most problematic answer, and indeed the ETA site gives good guidance on how to answer it.

But there's a further hidden problem: the form doesn't want slot-in answers for Nationality, Date of Birth, and Family name. It wants you to gather them from your passport, and it may delay your entry to Australia if your answers don't match your passport exactly. For most people the way the find the answers won't make any difference; their slot-in answers are the same as the gathered ones.

Spanish family names http://
klamath.stanford.edu/~molinero/
html/surname.html
Information on Icelandic surnames
http://eng.domsmalaraduneyti.is/
information/nr/125

But not for everyone. For example, many people with Spanish or other Hispanic names use more than one combination of their family names. Some people (e.g., most Icelanders) do not have a "family name" as such. And for the native of the UK, our nationality in our passports is "British Citizen" not "UK Citizen" – and the slot-in answer might be "Scottish" or "Welsh."

Know where users will find answers

There's only one way to be really certain about where users will find answers to your questions: ask some of them. Look out especially for questions with mismatches, where users actually need to use a different strategy to the one that you expect. Most importantly, don't assume that every answer will be slot-in.

Know who has the data you want

The purpose of your form is to get data from someone, but have you considered whether the person who has the answers is the same person as the person who fills in the form?

For example, we found that for the conference registration about half the delegates fill in the registration themselves, but the remainder get someone else to do it for them: the purchasing department of their organizations or the person who handles the training budget.

If you are looking at moving an existing paper form onto the Web, it is crucial to find out how the forms are completed at the moment and by whom. Some forms are completed by "real" end users. Other forms are completed on behalf of the end users. For example, they might be completed by

- Sales representatives;
- Help desk staff;
- An accountant;
- A secretary;
- A friend or relative.

We call these forms "hidden" forms. Problems often occur when organizations want to convert a "hidden" form to an online form. Problems that have been solved in the past by the intermediary are now pushed into the face of people who previously didn't complete them. They no longer have an intermediary to interpret your organization's terminology, product lists, ways of working, and all the other details that they've previously been shielded from.

For example, we worked with a telecommunications company that had specialized forms to enable customers to purchase and configure data services. In practice, however, customers never completed the forms. Instead, the sales representatives used their own forms to gather the information they needed and then completed the "official" forms for the customers back at their offices. They then faxed the completed form to the customers for signatures. The customers did not understand the "official" forms at all. Putting the forms on the Web so that customers could fill them in themselves would have been a disaster.

Help users to find the answers

Think about how users will find the answers and design your questions around that. Consider this form for ordering flowers from 1800flowers.com. It's packed with help for finding different answers.

This is a slot-in answer, but the site still makes it easy to find the exact details of your usual recipients.

This could be slot-in, but foreign or unfamiliar addresses might need to be gathered. The site makes it easy to find.

This could be slot-in or created. The drop-down makes it clear what choices are available.

This is likely to be slot-in, but the user could be thinking "on Saturday" or "as soon as possible." The "Tomorrow" link and calendar are helpful.

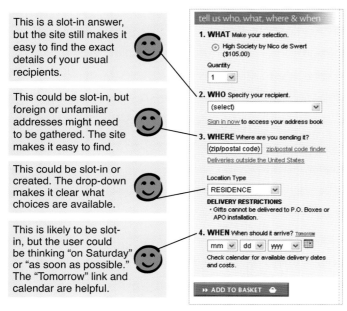

1800flowers.com offers a lot of help for finding the answer.

And 1800flowers.com even offers help for an answer that's definitely created: the message for the gift card.

Even a created answer may need some help, and here's a selection of samples.

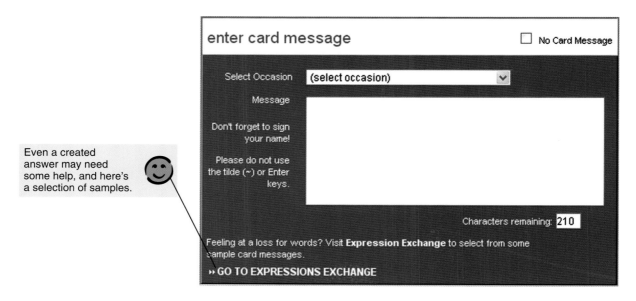

If your users will have to gather answers from paperwork that you send to them, you can help them by giving them a picture of where to find the answer.

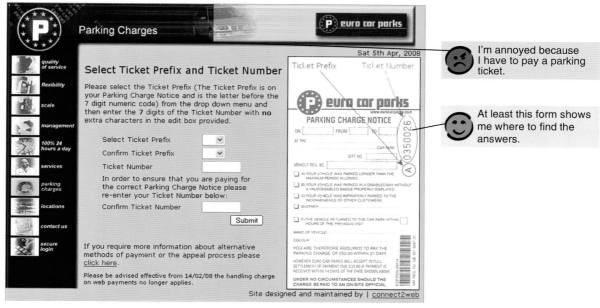

Euro car parks offers help for finding a gathered answer.

Write labels that match ways users find the answers

Although your form is asking questions, you don't need a fully formed, grammatical question or request for each field.

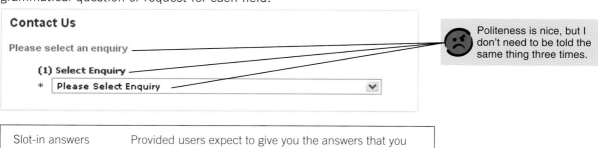

Slot-in answers	Provided users expect to give you the answers that you want, you can reduce your labels to a brief prompt.
Gathered answers	A brief prompt is likely to be OK. May benefit from help about how to find the answer.
Third-party answers	Extra effort is required from the user. Likely to need a proper question to explain what is needed. Think about whether you should be sending the form to someone else.
Created answers	Likely to need a proper question. Think about providing help to structure or constrain the answer.

Make it easy to judge the answer

"Judging the answer" is our term for the process of deciding whether the answer in your head fits with the overall relationship and this specific question. The effort of judging varies considerably.

Let's check out someone signing up for Digg.com. As the website puts it, "Digg is a place for people to discover and share content from anywhere on the web." Our user is a typical Internet professional; she has her own website, uses several email accounts, and maintains a professional life on the Web. But she also enjoys using the Web for her personal interests and social life. She has several different usernames and passwords that she reserves for different purposes.

The start of Digg.com's registration form

These thoughts might never be expressed, or even thought in such detail. But judgment processes like these are going on all the time as people answer questions—or they should be.

Sometimes people may not realize how their answers will be interpreted. For example, job applicants may not see a curriculum vitae (CV) or application form as providing the ability to express their goals and personality. They need to be reminded to judge their answer from the point of view of a prospective employer.

LinkMe (www.linkme.com.au), a resume listing site, reminds users to judge their answers from an employer's point of view.

Avoid privacy errors: Explain why you want to know the answer

Privacy errors happen when the user has an answer available but doesn't want to tell you it. Privacy errors are a failure at the stage of judging the answer. You can reduce them by providing an explanation of why you want the answer:

- The explanation must be truthful.
- The user must believe the explanation.
- And the user must want to achieve whatever you're using as your justification (so make sure you've thought about user goals).

Your explanation doesn't have to be complicated. This registration form deals with a privacy error in one short sentence.

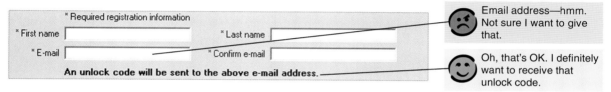

This part of a registration form asks for email but justifies why the user should reveal that answer.

Make it easy to put the answer on the form

The final step in answering the question is putting the answer on the form. The most flexible way to do that is to offer users a box to type into, but often you want to help the user by offering the most likely answers as a set of choices. Or perhaps your investigations of how you'll use the data showed that only a few specific answers can be handled.

We'll go into more detail on how to choose controls such as type-in boxes or radio buttons in Chapter 5.

Match the options you offer to the ones in users' minds

Sometimes the options have a set of commonly used values, as in the following snippet from the registration form:

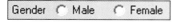

The registration form offers a standard selection of genders.

Most of us would find these usual two options acceptable, although you can get a t-s hirt that challenges them.

No Pity Shirts sells a t-shirt with a different selection of gender categories. (www.nopityshirts.com)

Digg.com offers an even wider choice.

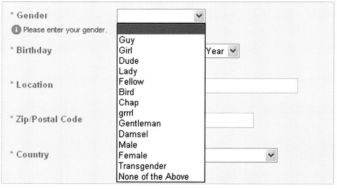

Digg.com offers the most comprehensive set of options for gender that we have seen so far.

But too often we come across forms where the options on offer don't match the answer that we have. For most of us, the country we're in would be a slot-in answer. But that doesn't stop the option errors as you can see here.

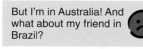

And sometimes the real world is just more complex than the form designer allows for. What if:

- more than one option applies?
- some options overlap?
- we don't understand the explanation offered?

In this registration form, the options are complex, and there's no choice for "more than one."

There's one simple solution to most option errors:

- Offer "other" as one of your choices.

Put the "other" option at the bottom of the list so that the users can see it easily after they've rejected all the other ones.

Ideally, you should include a box so that the users can say what "other" it is that they want to tell you about. Then you can check your data to find out whether you have missed some common option or whether the "other" choices really are unusual.

Summary: Making questions easy to answer

In this chapter, we went through the four steps of answering a question:

1. Understand the question.
2. Find the answer.
3. Judge the answer.
4. Put the answer on the form.

To make these steps as easy as possible:

- Ask about concepts that the users are familiar with, using words that they understand.
- Think about how users find the answer. Should you offer help about where an answer could come from?
- Think about whether users will want to answer. Is this the right moment in the relationship to ask this question?
- And think about forcing users into your options. Could you offer an "other" option to cater for the unexpected?

Writing Useful Instructions

4

Write useful instructions

In the preceding chapter, we looked at questions. No questions, no form: simple as that.

But many forms contain plenty of writing that isn't questions: introductory discussion (we call this "preamble"), help, terms and conditions, and so on. For convenience, we'll refer to these as "instructions."

Some instructions are necessary for legal reasons. We're not insured for your legal problems, so do what your lawyers tell you (but try to make sure even the legal material is as simple and short as possible).

If you're interested in making legal language simple, then join Clarity, the lawyers' association for plain language. www.clarity-international.net

Some instructions are helpful:

- a good title that says what the form is for;
- a list of anything that users might have to gather to answer the questions;
- something that tells users how to get help;
- a thank-you message at the end that says what will happen next.

Maybe a hundred words altogether?

Now take a look at the instructions on your form. Aside from the legal, what do you have left? A hundred words? More like a thousand? Or pages of it?

If you'd like more information on writing for the Web, the definitive book is *Letting Go of the Words* by Janice (Ginny) Redish (2007). Her work has inspired us for years.

Most of us have far too much. That's a problem because no one likes instructions and everyone tries to avoid reading them.

In this chapter, we work through a three-step checklist for sorting out instructions:

1. Rewrite them in plain language.
2. Cut the ones that aren't needed.
3. Move them to where they are needed.

Rewrite instructions in plain language

We find that instructions come at us from all sorts of different technical specialists. They're concentrating on the subject matter, not clear writing. It's up to us to get the instructions into plain language.

Plain language rule 1: Use familiar words in familiar ways

Use familiar words

There are lists of the most common words that you can use as a starting point. For example, there is Basic English, described by Charles K. Ogden in the 1930s. This is a set of 850 simple words that should be understood by most learners of English, plus a further set of 2,000 words that should be understood by more advanced learners.

The speedy way to find out whether you are using familiar words is to submit your text to a vocabulary checking program.

The following text has "???" for each word that is outside the most common 2,000. We think that it is possible to work out the gist of this text, but it looks likely to be challenging for users with a limited vocabulary.

We learned about Basic English from the web site: ogden.basicenglish.org/

We use "Vocab Profile" at www.lextutor.ca/vp. This shows whether words are among the most common 2,000.

What is the baby ???

The baby ??? is a ??? tax ???—even if you do not pay tax, do not have any ??? or do not have to ??? a tax return you can still claim it. The baby ??? is paid whether or not you currently get any other family ???.

Who is it for?

If you had a baby or you gained ??? responsibility of a child aged under five (for example, through adoption), on or after 1 July 2001 and before 1 July 2004—whether or not you already have other children—you could receive the baby ???. Usually, it is the mother of the child who is ??? for the baby ???.

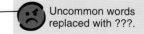

Uncommon words replaced with ???.

Part of the opening instructions from the "Baby Bonus" calculator on a tax web site analyzed for uncommon words.

What is the baby bonus?

The baby bonus is a refundable tax offset – even if you do not pay tax, do not have any income or do not have to lodge a tax return you can still claim it. The baby bonus is paid whether or not you currently get any other family benefits.

Who is it for?

If you had a baby or you gained legal responsibility of a child aged under five (for example, through adoption), on or after 1 July 2001 and before 1 July 2004 – whether or not you already have other children – you could receive the baby bonus. Usually, it is the mother of the child who is eligible for the baby bonus.

The original text from the "Baby Bonus" calculator on a tax web site.

Use words in familiar ways

Even if a word is apparently familiar, it doesn't necessarily mean the same thing to everyone. Meaning can change geographically or by context.

In a geographical sense, you may have come across some variations in usage, such as a British "holiday" is an American "vacation." A "singlet" in Australia is a "vest" in the UK and an "undershirt" in the USA. The Australian sign "no thongs" outside a bar translates to "don't wear flip-flops" in U.S. English. In business, it's useful to know that if Americans "table" something in a meeting, they take if off the agenda, whereas if the British "table" something, they add it to the agenda.

In this context...	"Within the last week" may mean...
At work	Within the last five working days, or maybe the period from Monday to Friday last week
In a television program guide	Within the last seven days, or maybe the period from Sunday to Saturday last week
In this context...	**"Frequent" may mean...**
A headache	One a week
A heart attack	One a year

And one of our favorites:

- If you ask for "title" before name, it means "salutation" (Mr., Mrs., and Ms. are the most common).
- If you ask for "title" after name, it often means "job title."
- If you ask for "title" without any name, it is likely to mean "book title" or "movie title."

Plain language rule 2: Use short, affirmative, active sentences

"Short" sentences are up to 20 words long.

"Affirmative" sentences are positive, not negative.

"Active" sentences are in the active voice: it's clear who is doing what. People who don't have English as their first language find active sentences much easier to read.

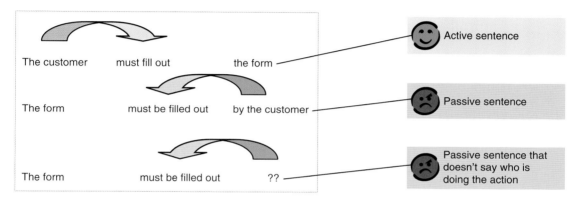

From Redish (2007).

"Terms and conditions" frequently contain nasty examples of sentences that break rule 2. Example:

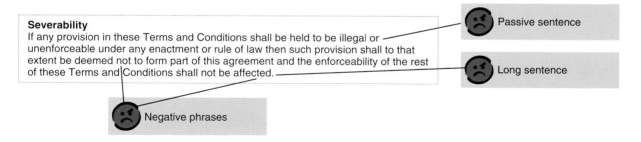

We think this means:

Severability
If a court rules that something in these Terms and conditons is illegal or unenforce-able, then we will act as if that part of the Terms and Conditions was deleted. The rest of the Terms and Conditions will not be affected.

But we're not sure. That's why we need Plain Language Rule 2.

Plain language rule 3: Demolish walls of words

"Walls of words"—big blocks of unbroken text—are demoralizing for users. Organize your text so that it is in meaningful chunks. Make good use of white space, bullet points, and tables.

We worked with www.loanbright.com, a business that provides mortgage quotations. Here's the original text of the preamble to the company's form.

All those words! I feel daunted already. I'm out of here.

Request a Personalized Rate Quote

Tired of calling a list of mortgage providers only to be asked the same questions over and over again? Let our lenders and brokers come to you! By providing the following information, one or more companies in your area will provide a "personalized quote" on your borrowing request. Most will respond in less than 24 hours. Please complete this form as thoroughly as possible.

This text looked like a "wall of words," so we persuaded Loanbright to chop it up into smaller pieces.

Here's the version that the company tried next:

Request a Personalized Rate Quote

About Us | Privacy Statement | Contact Us

This mortgage rate quote form will take approximately 30 seconds to complete. Here's how our service works:

- Complete our short form
- We will search hundreds of mortgage lenders and thousands of loan programs in our database
- You will then receive quotes from up to 4 competitive lenders in your state
- You choose the mortgage lender with the best rate and loan terms and save money!

OK, I've been able to read the instructions in a couple of seconds. Maybe I'll try the rest of the form.

The changes aren't all that dramatic, are they? But the effect on Loanbright's business really was important. The company increased its conversion rate (percentage of people who visit this page and then go on to complete the form) by 33%.

(We wanted Loanbright to take out the sentence about how long it would take to complete because we don't think it's necessary. But the staff liked it, for this form it really is truthful, and it doesn't seem to be doing any harm to the conversion rate.)

Plain language rule 4: Put choices before actions

Peter Dixon is a cognitive psychologist whose interests include the problem of how people read and understand different types of instructions. He ran an experiment (Dixon, 1987) where people had to follow simple pairs of drawing instructions. Each of them had a "choice" instruction describing the aim of the picture and an "action" instruction describing how to draw it.

Here's an example: *"Draw a triangle above an upside-down T. This will be a picture of a wine glass."*

A significant number of participants drew something like this:

Because the "action" (draw a triangle) came first, participants skipped the "choice" (draw a wine glass).

When the sentences are changed around—*"This will be a picture of a wine glass. Draw a triangle above an upside-down T"*—participants didn't make the same mistake; they decided what to draw before undertaking the action:

We don't ask people filling in forms to draw many diagrams. But we do, again and again, expect them to follow instructions with a choice and an action.

"If choice then do action" constructions are fine.

"Do action if choice" constructions are risky. Some people will do the action without making the choice, even if both bits seem almost trivially easy.

 Action is here.   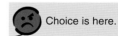 Choice is here.

Alternate application versions can be used in the event an applicant chooses to provide slightly different information to one institution from another institution. Below are the steps necessary to create an alternate version.

Let's turn around the opening sentence above, replacing the hidden "if" ("in the event") with a real "if":

"If you choose to provide slightly different information to one institution from another institution, then you can use alternate versions of your application."

Now we can decide whether or not we might need alternate versions.

Plain language rule 5: Use helpful headings

See Bartell, Schultz, and Spyridakis (2006). Also see our commentary "Good Headings Help—Bad Headings Hurt" www.usabilitynews.com/news/article3666.asp

Headings help to structure your text. Readers skip and skim to the places that seem relevant to them. You cannot stop them doing it, so you may as well point the way so that they do, in fact, pick the places that are relevant to them.

Recent research has found that putting in headings at arbitrary intervals doesn't help. So don't create rules like "include a heading after every second paragraph."

Headings are good if they:

- guide users through your text;
- match the goals that users have;
- break the text at appropriate points.

One quick way to find out whether your headings are working is to look at them in isolation from the rest of the text.

This set of headings from a privacy policy is a mixture of good and bad.

Writing good headings seems obvious—but doesn't always happen.

On the next page, we've put the contents pages from the instructions for two sets of comparable complex forms: university applications, listing the headings.

Think about being a 17-year-old who is about to apply to a university. Which set of headings do you think work best for the student? Which are more about the organization's goals than the student's?

contents

You can get copies of this guide in large print if you are partially sighted. Ask your school or college to contact us for a copy, or contact our Customer Service Unit on 0870 1122211.

Contents

Contacting the OUAC

Please read the entire instruction booklet before proceeding.
It is the applicant's responsibility to ensure that the application material and the required fees are received by the OUAC before the deadlines published herein.

Submit only one application. There are NO refunds.

Applications and supporting documents are used only for the year specified. A new application is produced annually.

Inquiries
Applicant Services: (519) 823-1940, extension 556

Mailing Address
Ontario Universities' Application Centre
170 Research Lane
Guelph ON N1G 5E2

Contents pages from two university application forms:
joint application to all UK universities (left); contents page for all Ontario, Canada, universities (right).

Cut instructions that aren't needed

Once users have clicked to fill in a form, they don't want fluff.

They don't want sales pitches (they've passed that point and are now focused on completing the form). Limit yourself to the briefest of statements about what users can achieve by filling in the form. Link them back to the sales pitch if you like.

They don't want to be told it will be "easy and quick." If the form is genuinely easy, the users can just get on with it. If it isn't, you've undermined the users' confidence straight away.

We also cut out claims about how long filling in the form will take. Such claims may be worthwhile if it really is a beast of a form and users should be aware of that: "This form will take you at least three hours to complete. Pack a lunch." But for the odd 5 or 10 minutes here or there, is it really necessary to waste valuable seconds telling users about it?

eBay's opening instructions summarize all you need to know into one short sentence.

Put instructions where they are needed

So far, we've been looking at all the instructions just as writing.

Now it's time to think about them in the context of being associated with a form. At the start of this chapter, we mentioned that some instructions are helpful:

- a good title that says what the form is for;
- a list of anything that users might have to gather to answer the questions;
- something that tells users how to get help;
- a thank-you message that says what will happen next.

The title and list of things to gather need to go at the beginning, the help in the middle, and the thank-you message at the end.

Include a title that says what the form is for

It's reassuring for users to see a title that reflects the purpose of the form. They won't always arrive at the form in a predictable way, and a good clear title is also helpful for search engine optimization.

We try to avoid titles with the word "Form" in them. Filling in the form is the barrier to whatever you want the form to do for you; it's best not to emphasize the point.

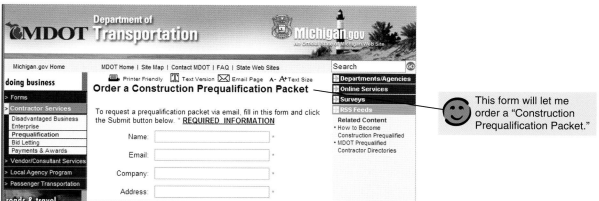

If you're not a construction contractor in Michigan, you're probably not familiar with the phrase "Construction Prequalification Packet." But that's OK: in Plain Language Rule 1, we said "use familiar words in familiar ways"—familiar for the target users, not necessarily for everyone.

Put a list of things to gather at the front of the form

If your users will have to hunt around for documents or other information, it's helpful to let them know that up front.

Clear step that tells you what to do before you begin

Would be even better if you could easily see that there are four items here (looks like seven)

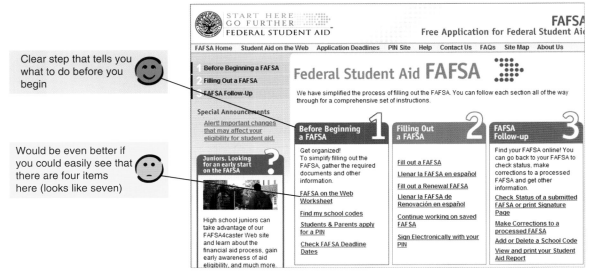

Users filling in this complex form need to gather a lot of information.

Don't bother telling users in advance that they will need to fill in slot-in answers; they already have that information in their heads, that's why they are slot-in answers. You may need to justify why you need the slot-in answers, but that justification needs to go at the point where you ask the question. In the following example, the justification comes too early.

The senator didn't need to tell me in advance about these slot-in answers: whether I want a response, and name and address.

Users using this form to contact a senator don't need to do anything special in advance.

It's OK to guide users to a different form

Sometimes you have to send users to a different form, like in this one from the City of Redmond.

Redmond does a nice job of explaining when you should use a different form.

Ideally, you would solve this sort of problem by having different links on the page that got you to the form. But we can't rely on users getting to the form by the route we planned, so it's OK to have a sentence to get them to the right form if this one isn't it.

It's good to replace instructions with questions

Another, and better, way of solving the problem of sending people to another form is to turn the instructions that guide them there into questions. And often, the instructions are full of words that would be better as questions, forcing people to consider them.

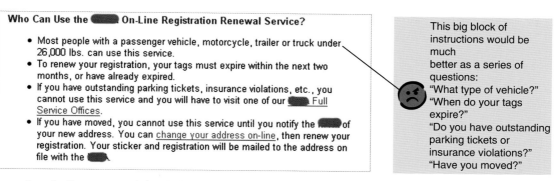

This big block of instructions would be much better as a series of questions: "What type of vehicle?" "When do your tags expire?" "Do you have outstanding parking tickets or insurance violations?" "Have you moved?"

This form asks whether a complaint being submitted is about users' "personal health records." If so, the users will be redirected to another government agency:

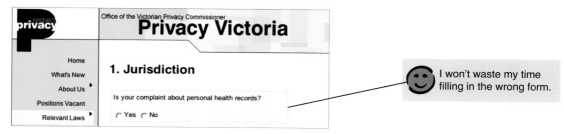

I won't waste my time filling in the wrong form.

A "before and after" example

We thought we'd try it all on one short form.

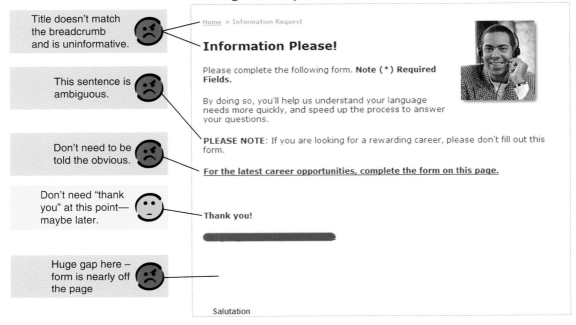

Title doesn't match the breadcrumb and is uninformative.

This sentence is ambiguous.

Don't need to be told the obvious.

Don't need "thank you" at this point—maybe later.

Huge gap here – form is nearly off the page

Home > Information Request

Information Please!

Please complete the following form. **Note (*) Required Fields.**

By doing so, you'll help us understand your language needs more quickly, and speed up the process to answer your questions.

PLEASE NOTE: If you are looking for a rewarding career, please don't fill out this form.

For the latest career opportunities, complete the form on this page.

Thank you!

Salutation

Our "after" version is just as friendly but gets straight to the point.

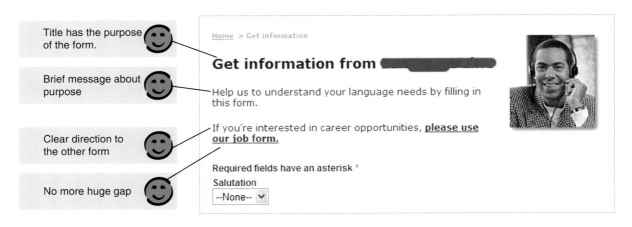

Title has the purpose of the form.

Brief message about purpose

Clear direction to the other form

No more huge gap

Home > Get information

Get information from

Help us to understand your language needs by filling in this form.

If you're interested in career opportunities, **please use our job form.**

Required fields have an asterisk *
Salutation
--None--

Summary: Writing instructions

A few well-positioned instructions can really help your form. Hundreds of complex words will definitely hurt it.

Start by making sure that your instructions are in plain language:

- Use words that your target users are familiar with.
- Use simple sentences in the active voice.
- Get rid of big blocks of text.
- Put choices before actions: "If" before "then."
- Remember that good headings help, bad headings hurt.

Then review your instructions to make sure that you have only the useful ones and that they are in the right place:

At the start of the form, you need to do the following:

- Include a title that says what the form is for.
- If you have gathered answers, then provide a list of things to gather.
- If some people should use a different form, then send them off to it.

But don't put things that happen at the end of the form at the beginning.

Here's a dilemma: You have a complex form, you've done your very best to avoid the need for help, but you know that some users will need it. On the other hand, you've heard that users are reluctant to click on "Help." What to do?

Provide help where it's needed

Make sure that help is in a position where people can find it readily.

Users focusing on filling in the form won't see this help up here

Change of major is an important decision; it's great that help is available.

But why are the two types of help separated?

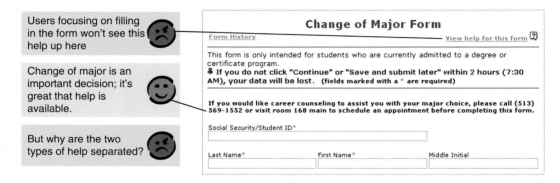

If the form has only the occasional difficult field, then it makes sense to place a link that says exactly what help you will get next to the field itself.

Instead of saying "help," this link entices by solving the user's immediate problem.

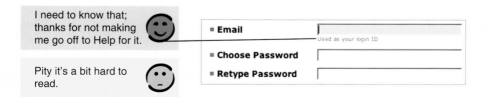

User Interface Engineering's credit card form puts help where it is needed.

If you can, write help that is short enough to be placed right next to the field: an example, an explanation, or details of how the answer will be used.

I need to know that; thanks for not making me go off to Help for it.

Pity it's a bit hard to read.

Email
Used as your login ID

Choose Password

Retype Password

Don't repeat yourself

Sometimes we see forms in which someone has been told to write help for every field—even when it doesn't make sense to do so.

Location
Please enter either the exact location or describe the location details for your request.

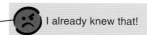 I already knew that!

If you find yourself writing this sort of text, you might want to rethink your help strategy so that you don't make users trudge through this sort of redundant information. Perhaps you don't need help for every field?

Separate instructions from background and other information

When users are following instructions, it is confusing to have to deal with extraneous information. Users who are looking for help don't want marketing "fluff" or lengthy explanations of policy or legal background.

The following example suffers from several problems, including poor layout. Items 1 and 2 are instructions, while item 3 is background information ("All future communications will be sent to the address indicated in this field").

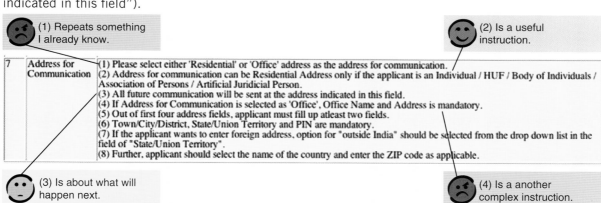

(1) Repeats something I already know.

(2) Is a useful instruction.

7	Address for Communication	(1) Please select either 'Residential' or 'Office' address as the address for communication. (2) Address for communication can be Residential Address only if the applicant is an Individual / HUF / Body of Individuals / Association of Persons / Artificial Juridicial Person. (3) All future communication will be sent at the address indicated in this field. (4) If Address for Communication is selected as 'Office', Office Name and Address is mandatory. (5) Out of first four address fields, applicant must fill up atleast two fields. (6) Town/City/District, State/Union Territory and PIN are mandatory. (7) If the applicant wants to enter foreign address, option for "outside India" should be selected from the drop down list in the field of "State/Union Territory". (8) Further, applicant should select the name of the country and enter the ZIP code as applicable.

(3) Is about what will happen next.

(4) Is a another complex instruction.

The mixing of two types of information means that you have to read everything before you can act appropriately.

Our version of this instruction is

Address for Communication	We will send all future correspondence to this address.
	If you are an Individual, HUF, Body of Individuals, Association of Persons, or Artificial Juridicial Person, then you can choose Residential or Office.
	If you are anyone else, you must choose Office.
	Make sure that the address is a complete postal address.
	If outside India, include country and ZIP code if applicable.

Don't lose users in large files

If your form is long, then you'll be splitting it up into sections or pages:

- Try to make sure that you split up the help in the same way.
- Avoid throwing users into the middle of a long help file.
- Definitely do not deliver users to the top of the file and expect them to find their own way to the relevant section.

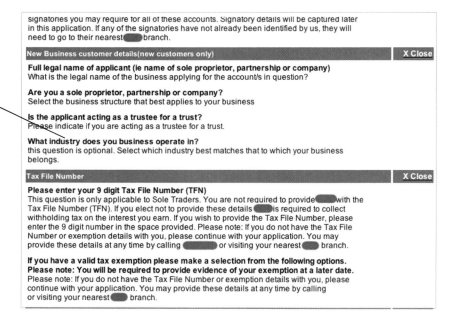

What section was I in?
I'll get lost as I scroll up
and down.

Allow users to escalate

Sometimes a help document is just not enough. The explanations may not be clear enough, or special circumstances may apply. Again and again in usability testing and field observations, we see users look for telephone numbers so that they can call on real human assistance.

Providing a phone number or, at a minimum, help request form or email address can help meet these needs (and also show that your organization is committed to its users).

Choosing Forms Controls

5

Choose appropriate controls

It's not enough for a user simply to have an answer in mind when responding to a form: The answer is no good until the user has got it into the form by typing, clicking, or whatever.

Wroblewski, 2008 has great discussion of the problem of choosing input fields, including a perspective from Bob Baxley

Often, a moment's thought about what the majority of users will want to convey in their answers is enough to guide you to the correct choice of control.

Occasionally, it's not quite so obvious which control to use, or you find yourself in an argument with someone who thinks that "drop-downs are user friendly" and so insists on using them everywhere.

You can ask a few questions that will help you think about your choice of control:

- Is it more natural to type rather than select?
- Are the answers easily mistyped?
- How many options are there?
- Is the user allowed to select more than one option?
- Are the options visually distinctive?
- Does the user need to see the options to understand the question?

And we'll also think a bit about the use of specialist controls such as calendars.

Meet users' expectations about how controls work

Users come to your form with experience of thousands of previous online interactions. In the following table we've listed the five most common controls and provided an example of how each might be used to allow a user to answer the same question.

Control	An example, using a choice of hotel room	How users expect it to work
Drop-down box	Single room ▼ Single room Twin room Double room	View a default choice. Click on down arrow to show choices. Scroll through list if necessary. Click on one option to select it. One of the options could be blank or labeled "other." A few users might expect to be able to hold down the Ctrl key and make multiple selections (but most would not).
Radio (option) buttons	◉ Single room ○ Twin room ○ Double room	View default choice. If not acceptable, click on another option to select it. Users would expect to be able to select only one option.
Checkboxes	☑ Single room ☐ Twin room ☐ Double room	Click on all acceptable choices. Can leave all the boxes blank if none are acceptable.
The type-in box	Single room	Type in a response or leave the box blank.
Links	<u>Single room</u> <u>Twin room</u> <u>Double room</u>	Click on one link to see a new page.

We've included links as a way for users to convey the answers in their heads through actions. Do you agree?

Is it more natural to type rather than select?

Slot-in answers such as name, address, and date of birth-are so well known to us that it is much easier and more natural to type them in directly rather than selecting from a list.

Think about booking a hotel room. You'd probably expect to type your name: How else would the hotel staff know if you've never stayed there before? But for "type of room," you'd need to know what the hotel is offering.

We often hear of a particular annoyance in the United States: being forced to select your two-letter state abbreviation from a 50-state drop-down. And yet, most people who live in the United States find it perfectly natural to type this (and are unlikely to make a mistake when doing so).

But in Japan, it's much easier to select everything from a drop-down due to the difficulty of typing Japanese kanji.

Japanese writing

Japanese uses all these ways of writing:

Kanji	More than 50,000–200,000 pictographic or ideographic characters.
Hiragana	About 100 phonographic characters.
Katakana	A different set of phonographic characters used for foreign names and words.
Alphabet	Acronyms, initial words, and some easy English (or other European) words to express "Western feelings."
Numbers	0123456789

Suppose you want the kanji 橋, pronounced "hasi."

- You first type "ha" (using alphabetic characters) and get it converted to Hiragana は(ha).
- Then you type "si" and get it converted to し(si).

There are several Japanese words pronounced "hasi." (English also has many words that are pronounced the same but mean different things: think of "rose" or "stock"). The system now offers you a drop-down with all the kanji it knows that might fit your requirements.

You choose the one you want and move on to your next word.

(Thanks to Manabu Ueno for this explanation.)

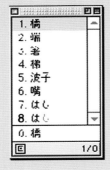

Are the answers easily mistyped?

Some answers are easy to mistype.

For example, although the hotel staff are likely to type the full, official name of a hotel correctly ("Cheviot Country Hotel and Golfing Center"), a user booking a room on the web might easily make a mistake by spelling it differently or by using an abbreviation that differs from the hotel's own preference (e.g., "Cheviot Golf Center").

Sometimes this type of mistake doesn't matter, but if it does, then it's probably best to avoid type-in boxes. The Ritz-Carlton provides a drop-down to help users avoid problems of misspelling and mistyping.

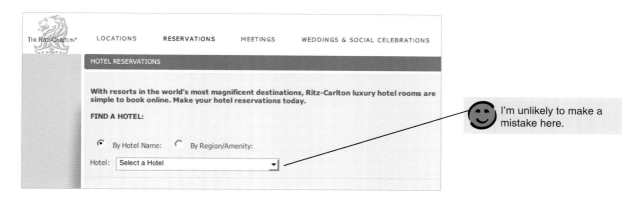

Hyatt allows users to type hotel names but also has a strategy for dealing with misspellings.

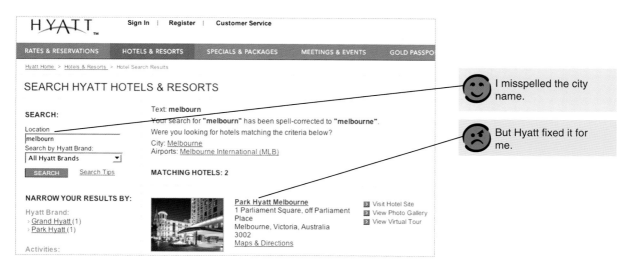

How many options are there?

Where there are very few options (four or fewer), radio buttons or checkboxes work better than a drop-down box. The users can see all options at a glance, it takes one click to make a choice and, with so few options, space on the page is not an issue.

Sometimes, though, dealing with options is a bit trickier. For example, think about expiration date of the credit card. There are only 12 months in a year, and it's probably sensible to offer up to 10 years in advance. But that's still quite a lot to scroll through. We're always surprised that so many credit card forms opt for drop-downs. Why not go for a type-in box instead?

In the following example, business rules mean that only two invoices can ever be outstanding, so forcing users to type an invoice number (and amount) when this could be a drop-down or radio button is annoying.

Why is this form asking me to type in an invoice number when there's only one that needs to be paid?

And the form allows only a few types of credit cards. A set of radio buttons would show me which ones I can use.

Invoice No:

Amount:

Card Type: - Enter Type -

Card Number:

One way of solving the problem of too many options to scroll through is to be selective. Instead of offering a list of 170 countries or more, try offering a list of the countries that you currently do business with, plus "Other."

And, of course, long lists of options are particularly prone to errors where the list on offer doesn't include the answer the user has in mind.

Is the user allowed to select more than one option?

Where users are stating preferences, more than one response may be acceptable. Most users know that checkboxes allow for multiple selections.

If you want to avoid the problem of writing instructions to tell the users about multiple choices, or if you think your users will have problems with the choices, then you can offer radio buttons instead with an extra button for "any" or "all". This has the added advantage of letting users make multiple selections quickly, as shown in this example.

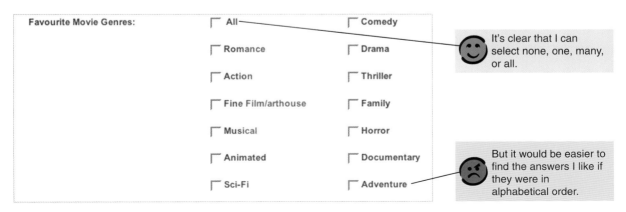

Are the options visually distinctive?

Scanning a list of options is easier if they are visually distinctive. For example, the following list has visually distinct letter forms, so it is quite easy to scan:

- Single
- Double
- Twin

But other options are not as easy to scan. For example, in this list of years for "Birthday," they are all rather similar, and if you're scrolling up and down quickly, it's rather easy to miss the one that you're interested in.

Whizzing up and down a long list of years is annoying. Why can't I just type it in?.

If your options look similar, then consider a type-in box in preference to offering users a list.

If you need to offer a list, then consider varying or abbreviating the options in some way so that it is easier to pick out each item. For example, if a chain of hotels shares similar names, then it might be better to offer a list of hotel locations instead.

Does the user need to see the options to understand the question?

The user may not know what the question is asking until the list of options is available.

For example, questions such as "Type of room" vary a lot according to culture and the context of the question:

- single, double, twin;
- two queen beds, king-size bed;
- deluxe, executive, regular, or budget;
- smoking, nonsmoking;
- ground floor, higher floor;
- Western-style, Japanese-style.

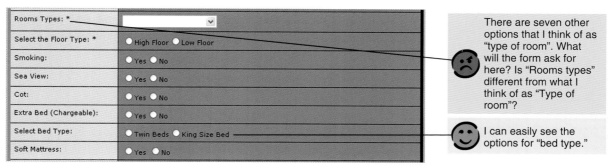

Sometimes, the question only makes sense in the context of the choices for the answer. If you use a drop-down, the choices are hidden until the user clicks. Using radio buttons or checkboxes shows the user instantly what the choices are.

Describe your options clearly

If you decide on a drop-down, radio buttons, or checkboxes, then you'll need a list of options as well as a label.

Options called "High floor" and "Low floor" are clear. It's easy to choose with confidence.

All these "yes"/"no" options aren't so good.

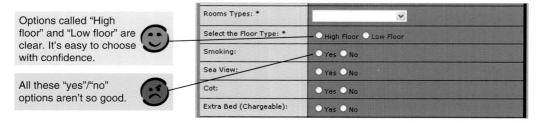

Using the actual answer as an option is better than providing a string of "yes"/"no" responses. But even the "yes"/"no" options are an improvement on the options under "Rooms Types."

I suppose I can guess that "Governor's Suite" will be the most expensive, but what am I paying for?

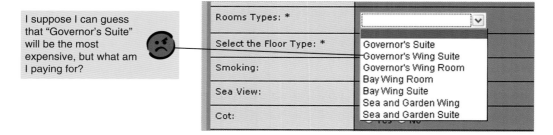

Choose a sensible order for the options

To enable visual scanning of the lists, order the options in a way that will make sense to the users. There may be a natural order to the options, for example, months of the year. In many other cases, sorting the options alphabetically makes it easy for the users to scan the list, although this doesn't always work, as you can see in the following screenshot.

It's hard to find Australian states when they're mixed up with U.S. ones.

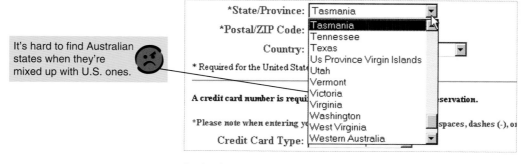

Sorting Australian and U.S. states together makes it harder for everyone.

Consider specialist controls—cautiously

So far, we have been choosing from the standard options for response spaces. The Web has moved on, so should we limit ourselves?

Broadly, we'd say *yes*. We like simple solutions that work on many different browsers. But there are also some good arguments for supplementing the standard controls with fancier ones.

Calendars help to show relative dates

Often, people aren't sure of exactly which date is required. For example, they might be thinking in terms of "tomorrow" or "the weekend before the holiday."

This section from a hotel booking site offers drop-downs for the date; a calendar plus type-in box would be easier.

A pop-up calendar can help, but you should make sure you always have another way of entering the date so that people who can't see the calendar are still able to use the form.

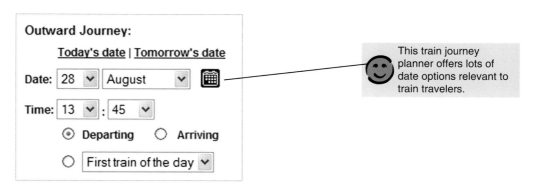

The UK's Network Rail allows for many ways that train travelers think of dates and times.

Maps help to show geography

If your users need to specify a geographical location, then a map is clearly a way to help them.

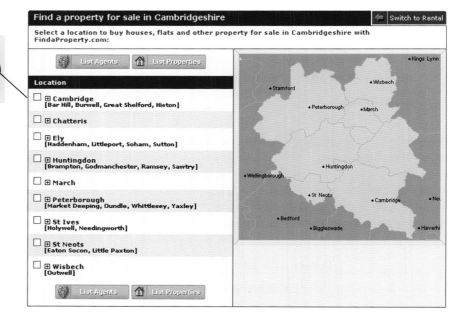

I'm looking for a property in a little English village in North Cambridgeshire, but these names mean nothing to me.

The form at www.findproperty.com lets me choose by text location or by clicking on a map.

We love maps, but we always offer a text alternative:

- Some people can't read maps or can't understand them.
- Some people won't be sufficiently familiar with the geography to know where to click.
- If the area you are interested in is small, (the classic example is Rhode Island on a map of the USA), then clicking on it can be hard.

Summary: Choosing controls

Although the standard choice of form controls on the web is limited, it is still possible to reach a dilemma over which element to use. Think about users' expectations of how the controls work.

- If typing the answer is more natural, then go for a type-in box.
- If users are likely to make mistakes when typing, then opt for something they can click.
- If there are a lot of options, using a drop-down may be best. But could you redesign the question instead?
- If the users are able to select more than one option, checkboxes are likely to be the best control.
- If the options all look alike, you may do better to let the users type into a text box instead.
- If the users need to see the options to understand the question, then radio buttons or checkboxes require less effort.

Drop-downs, radio buttons, and checkboxes all need options as well as labels. Describe your options clearly and choose a sensible order for the options.

Specialist controls such as calendars and maps have their place, but if you do use them, then make sure that you offer a plain text alternative.

Making the Form Flow Easily

Making the form flow easily

Spoken conversations have a natural flow. They switch from one topic to another. Sometimes one person says something that the other person doesn't understand. This confusion doesn't matter because in spoken language we are used to asking for clarifications or repeating parts of the conversation.

Asking for clarification is much harder when half of the conversation has been predefined, as it is in a form. So that's why we have to think about the topics, flow, and handling of errors in advance.

Break up long forms by topic

Ideally, a form would be a single screenful—easy enough to achieve if you need to ask only a few questions. But what do you do when you have dozens of questions?

If your form runs to more than about two screens long, you have two options:

1. Push all the fields close together and abbreviate the labels to pack everything into as few screens as possible.
2. Split your fields and labels across multiple pages.

Why two screens long? Because users often want to print forms for a variety of reasons, and two screens long will generally print OK on A4 or Letter-sized paper.

Crush the fields onto as few pages as possible (sometimes)

If your forms are used day-in, day-out by trained users, then those users will rapidly stop looking at the questions at all but instead look only at the data entry boxes. So for repetitive, daily-use forms, it makes sense to pack as much as possible onto the screen. But allow plenty of time for training.

For everyone else, crushing all the fields together to fit them onto a single page will make the form seem daunting. It's like shouting all your questions out at once.

Split across multiple pages by dividing the form into topics (better)

If you're working on a paper form, then each page has to be the same length. But on the Web, we have the flexibility to have longer and shorter pages according to topic. For example, your address is usually a single topic, so it's normal for U.S. forms to ask their U.S. customers for state and ZIP code on the same page. You'd need to have some special reason to justify splitting them.

We worked on a set of forms for Polish users to use every day. To help the British engineers configure the system, users could set a switch to show all the labels in Polish or in English. But after a couple of months, the Polish users didn't mind which language was showing; they had stopped reading the labels.

Very short pages seem to be OK if they are clearly about a single topic that is different from the one before and the one after. Don't feel that pages have to be a minimum length.

We have three suggestions for grouping into topics:

Keep to one topic at a time.	Jumping about between topics shows a lack of organization and a lack of attention.
Ask anticipated questions before surprising ones.	Users generally have ideas about what information they need to divulge. It's best to ask the anticipated questions before you move into something unexpected or unusual.
Ask less intrusive questions before more intrusive.	Ease into questions that may intrude on the user's privacy by dealing with neutral topics first.

Keep to one topic at a time

Here's a progress indicator for a job application form.

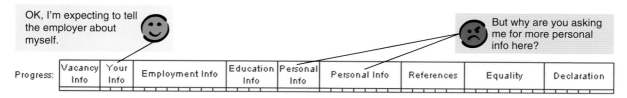

If a single topic is too big for one page, it's OK to split it across separate pages. But don't split the topic flow by interjecting anything else in between.

Breaking the conversation and the topic

We tested a form for a bank payment service on which the first page contained personal details such as name and telephone number. It also asked for country of residence (but not address).

The second screen had a warning message about the currency of the transactions being fixed by country of residence. Participants saw this as a change in the flow of the conversation and interpreted it as meaning "you've finished entering personal details."

The third screen asked for address. Several participants refused to give their address at this point, stating firmly that they had already done it.

Ask anticipated questions before surprising ones

In an ordinary conversation, we expect each new piece of information to relate to the information that has already been exchanged.

If the flow doesn't respect this convention, then it's disconcerting—or funny. Here's an example. This website invites the users to contact the organization for a free demo:

I'm interested in what this website offers, and I can get a free demo.

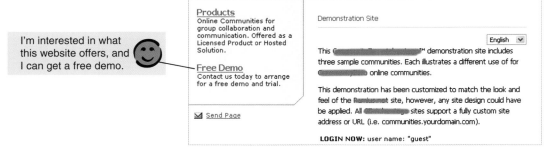

Since the user was told to "contact us... for a free demo," it seems reasonable to expect that the next page will be about contact details. Instead, the next question is "How did you first learn about..." the product. This question feels like a change of topic; it's off-putting and shows a lack of attention to detail.

This is not what I expected.

Axure also allows users to download a free trial but then asks that "unexpected" question at the end—but makes it optional.

My email address is required. All the other information is optional, and it comes after the question I expected.

Ask less intrusive questions before more intrusive

Often we want to start our form with "easy" questions—the ones with slot-in answers. That's fine if they fit in with the conversational flow of the form. But it's not fine if the question is unexpected, and especially not fine if the relationship hasn't developed far enough for the question to be acceptable.

Look at this "request music" form on the Apple iTunes website.

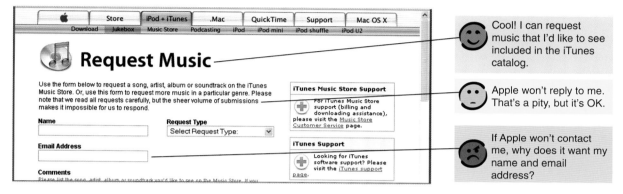

Cool! I can request music that I'd like to see included in the iTunes catalog.

Apple won't reply to me. That's a pity, but it's OK.

If Apple won't contact me, why does it want my name and email address?

If questions come up more than once, explain the difference between them

We recently received an email from an annoyed engineer: "I don't like the Cisco Tools registration. It started by asking for 'Language' twice!"

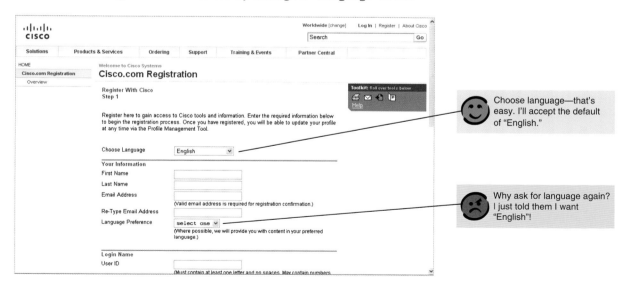

Choose language—that's easy. I'll accept the default of "English."

Why ask for language again? I just told them I want "English"!

"Choose language" and "Language preference" seem very much like asking the same question twice. Any ideas why this form does that?

We weren't sure. So we had a look.

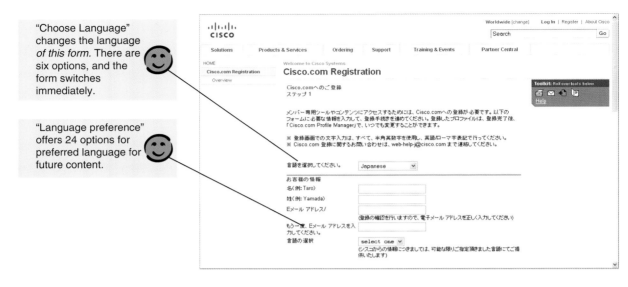

"Choose Language" changes the language *of this form.* There are six options, and the form switches immediately.

"Language preference" offers 24 options for preferred language for future content.

Cisco politely offers a selection of different languages for users to register in. Then it offers an even greater selection of languages for future communications. But not quite politely enough—as our engineer demonstrated.

Use progress indicators

If you'd like a longer discussion of progress indicators, try Wroblewski, 2008

A progress indicator is a graphic that shows the steps in the form and where you are along those steps.

Progress indicators are a good idea if:

- you can divide your form into a series of self-contained steps;
- you can predict how many steps users will go through;
- your form really does progress from one step to another;
- the answers are all slot-in or very easily gathered (so the form is completed in a single session).

The progress indicator on the Qantas site works well (and we like the cute airplane)

A good progress indicator:

- is honest, showing all the steps that you will go through;
- is updated as the user works through the form;
- uses a name or number or both (in addition to any images);
- is consistently named or numbered;
- is in the same place on each page of the form, preferably immediately above the questions.

Our user failed to notice the list of steps. They are over on the right side—not very noticeable when you're concentrating on the fields and labels.

Summary menus work better than progress indicators for some forms

Some forms don't really progress. Users have to tackle bits of them as they gather or research the answers.

For example, consider job applications. Users may need to check some dates or details for education or employment, so why not allow the users to tackle them in any order? And the problem is even worse if the form insists on every section being validated before the users can move on.

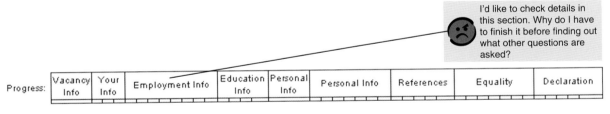

This job application form uses a summary menu and allows the users to choose to fill in the form in any order.

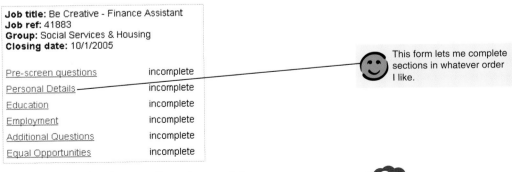

In this example, does "incomplete" mean there is mandatory information that the user needs to complete? Or should it also say "incomplete" if the user has left out optional questions?

For example, suppliers to the federal government in the United States are required to undertake Central Contractor Registration (CCR). This registration form is packed with gathered and third-party answers—a lot of work for users.

Recognizing the amount of work, the form doesn't have a progress indicator. Instead, it has a summary menu, which it calls "Registration Menu." As you work through several pages, each like the one shown here, a nice little menu updates itself, and you can click to jump around in the form as you find answers.

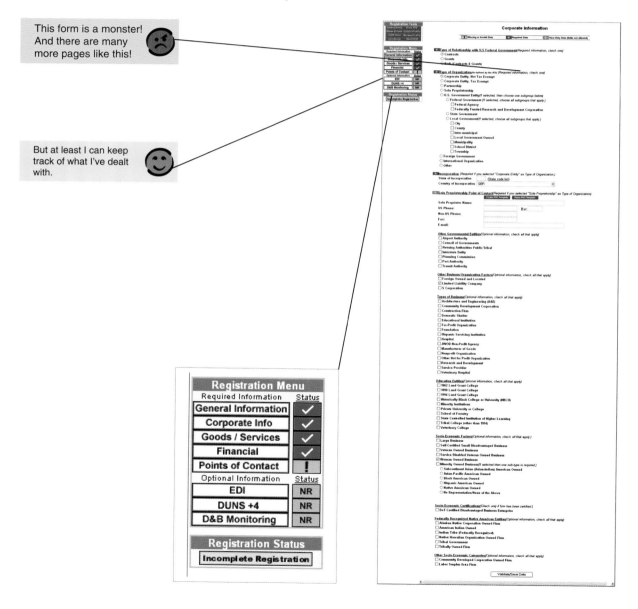

This form is a monster! And there are many more pages like this!

But at least I can keep track of what I've dealt with.

Don't surprise users with sudden changes

At the beginning of this chapter, we mentioned that in a web form, one side of the conversation is fixed. This is true—in the sense that the program is written in advance.

But it's also a simplification because one way of solving the problem of excessively long forms is to try to find ways of hiding questions from users depending on their previous answers. For example, a medical form might have a whole lot of questions that apply only to women and another set that applies only to men.

Avoid pages that change without warning

We've seen many forms that try to deal with this situation by dynamically changing the page as users answer questions. For example, look at this sequence.

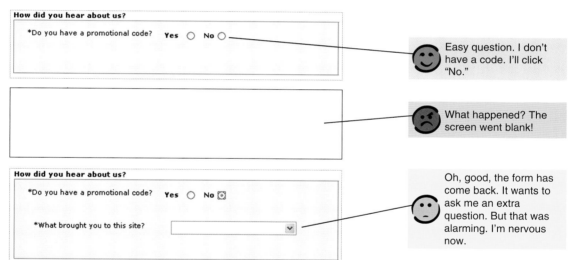

We've seen this momentary alarm again and again with dynamic screens. Novices become positively scared—not a good thing for a smooth flow through the form. But what has surprised us is that even very experienced Internet users give a little start as the screen changes on them. And if it goes completely blank, as in the example, they can get positively annoyed. We wonder why when this is becoming quite a common feature?

Thinking about the conversation helps to explain it. When a form page appears on the browser, the user assumes that this is the computer's contribution to the ongoing conversation. It has said its piece and will now wait quietly for the user to type. Suddenly changing the page breaks that conversational assumption. It's like someone asking you a question and then interrupting before you've finished your answer.

We've also seen the same effect on some of the fancier technologies for immediate validation. For example, consider these three screenshots.

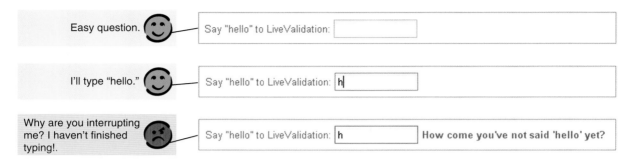

Easy question.

I'll type "hello."

Why are you interrupting me? I haven't finished typing!.

We'd like these ultra-speedy validations to work because immediate feedback should be a good idea. But they don't: They interrupt the conversational flow and disconcert users.

It's OK to change pages on user command

What we have seen working, very successfully, is a page that changes on user command.

For example, people in the UK know that their addresses can be identified easily from a postcode and a house number or name.

Easy question. I'll put in my postcode and click "get address."

And yes, the form is asking me for the rest of my address.

Clicking a command button, such as "get address," has the conversational effect of handing control back to the computer, which the user now *expects* to do something in response to the command.

It's OK to build a custom form based on earlier input

There's a natural command button on every page: the "Next" button that moves the user onto the next page. So one way to exploit the conversational turn-taking is to customize the next page based on answers for this page.

For example, we have seen successful forms that "prebuild" by using a small number of questions and then tailoring the form accordingly. Effectively, you're allowing the user to choose between multiple forms.

Australian Passport Application Forms

To determine which form you should complete, you will need to answer the following questions and then press the "Next" button.

BLANK FORMS CANNOT BE DOWNLOADED

Are you an Australian citizen? —————— ○ Yes ○ No

These questions are easy.

Are you in Australia?   ○ Yes ○ No

Do you wish to renew your Australian passport?   ○ Yes ○ No
(You can renew your adult passport if it has expired within the last twelve months. If you want to replace a Lost or Stolen Passport, you must answer "No")

Is this application for an adult or child?   ○ Adult ○ Child

One problem is that the crucial questions can appear almost random to the user and may not be a coherent topic. This problem can be solved by explaining why you're asking such questions at this point.

In the preceding Australian Passport example, there is an explanation about why the form is asking those questions.

We're not convinced about the value of this explanation because we think many users will focus just on the questions and miss the somewhat illegible explanation. What do you think?

Avoid tabs as a way of getting around a form

We often use tabs as a way of segmenting websites into different areas.

But we find that tabs don't work very well as a way of segmenting forms into topics. Once again, it's a problem of control. When a user clicks on the tab at the top, is that equivalent to a command button? Or not? Should changes made to that tab be applied? Or not?

And there's always a risk of overlooking the tab navigation altogether, with confusing results ("Where's the rest of the form?").

Luckily, we don't see tabs on forms very often these days. We don't use tabs to segment forms ourselves, and our searches for web form examples that use them were unsuccessful. It seems that most designers agree with us about avoiding them.

Be gentle with errors

Errors create another break in the smooth conversational flow of the form. We interrupt the peaceful user to say "you messed up."

Why is there an error in the first place? Here are some possible reasons:

Send errors	The user presses the "Send" button too early. Your server gets a page with many blank entries.
Typing errors	People sometimes hit the wrong key.
Transcription errors	A number is copied incorrectly, for example, when transferring it from a credit card. Transcription errors are frequently swaps or transpositions (the user types 4311 instead of 3411).
Category errors	The categories you offer do not match the answer that the user wants to give you.
Privacy errors	The question you have asked is inappropriate in context.

Validation helps some of the time

We don't want to collect bad data from our users, so we validate it. The challenge for usability is that validations help users to deal with send, typing, and transcription errors but may result in worse data for category and privacy errors. Especially privacy errors, where you may find that your supposedly "clean" data is full of people called Mickey Mouse who live in Afghanistan.

One way of finding out about category errors is to include "other" as a option everywhere you offer choices—at least for an initial trial period. You can then inspect the data to find out whether anyone is choosing "other." If not, you know that you aren't getting category errors.

We've often wondered about whether validating data at all is worthwhile—and certainly whether it is worth validating optional fields. Making this decision is a balance between three factors:

- the problem of having "clean" data in your database that is in fact rubbish;
- the problem of having "invalid" data in your database;
- the lack of respect that you would show if you simply discard the problematic data.

Could you offer a validation for the first attempt but allow users to continue anyway? We call these "soft validations" and seldom see them in web forms, but we know how useful they can be. For example, the software used to capture tax returns in the UK allows the user to override the validations when necessary. For example, there's a validation to catch entry of a currency amount over 10,000,000, which usually happens because the user has typed two entries into one box by mistake, but it is actually a correct entry for a few very wealthy individuals.

Validate as early as possible

Let's assume that you have carefully designed your form to avoid privacy and category errors. Validation will definitely help users with the other types.

Validate as early as possible after the user has finished typing the entry, but bear in mind the break you will cause in the conversational flow. Usually, this means that you will validate when the user has finished with a page.

If there are errors, make sure that the user is aware of them by redisplaying a page that:

- is clearly different to the one the user just submitted (we've often seen people confused by an apparent redisplay of the same page);
- has a prominent alert at the top;
- has a link to each error message, to help the user get to the error quickly (particularly important for those who use screen readers).

Then highlight each problem next to the field that caused it.

The form has told me about a problem

I see the problem.

Be polite:

- Assume that your users are trying their best.
- Don't use a patronizing or accusing tone.
- If possible, offer a suggestion about how to correct the error.
- If the error might be due to a privacy problem, explain why you need the data.
- If the error might be due to a category problem, explain why you have restricted the categories on offer.

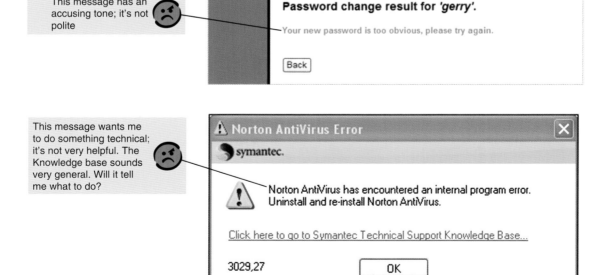

This message has an accusing tone; it's not polite

This message wants me to do something technical; it's not very helpful. The Knowledge base sounds very general. Will it tell me what to do?

Say "thanks" to close the conversation

Conversations should finish smoothly. When the user has finished the form, display a page that acknowledges the ongoing relationship:

- Provide a "thank you" or some other acknowledgment of the user's efforts.
- Make the page look as attractive as any other page on your site and ensure the message is legible.
- Let the user know what will happen next and make sure that you follow up as appropriate.
- Ensure that the page is printable or provide a "print-friendly" format.
- Offer a suitable next landing point within your website, such as being taken back to the home page.

Even if something goes wrong and you have bad news to impart, try to break it gently. Offer a contact for help and try to provide an error message in plain language, as well as the technical details that might help to solve the problem.

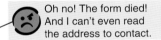

Summary: Making the form flow easily

A good conversation flows naturally from topic to topic. Exploit this to break up large forms into manageable chunks.

If your form includes some gathered or third-party answers, then find a good way of allowing users to store the form and come back to it, and opt for a summary menu rather than a progress indicator.

Avoid surprising users with sudden changes. If you need to be selective about what questions you present to users, then build pages that reflect their earlier answers.

Be gentle with errors. Validations may help guide users to correct input, but they may also force incorrect (or even downright stupid) answers out of reluctant users and undermine the relationship.

Be as careful with the final "thank you" or acknowledgment page as with the rest of your site. Even if you have to break bad news to the user, try to be as helpful as possible while doing it.

Do you remember the old days on the Web when we'd watch participants struggle because they didn't know about scrolling? And they'd click on a link only if it were blue and underlined?

At that time, and up to about 2000, the rule for pop-ups was simple: "Pop-ups: just say NO."

A year or so later, we started to notice that pop-ups weren't confusing our participants. Providing the pop-up conformed to certain rules, it was just fine. After some email discussion with Carl Zetie, we formulated the "Jarrett-Zetie Rules of Pop-ups."

The Jarrett-Zetie Rules of Pop-ups

Expectation	The user expects new content and expects that content to be a diversion from the current task rather than intrinsic to it.
Context	There is some advantage to the user in seeing the new content on screen at the same time as the existing content.
Size	The pop-up size is between one quarter and one third of existing window size. (If the size is less than one quarter, then the content should be moved onto the main page. If the size is more than one third, then you break the rule of context.)
Knowledge	The user isn't thrown by pop-ups and knows how to close them.
Obvious Single Use	There is only one pop-up at a time, and you have some way of being sure that the pop-up comes to the front.

Pop-ups are hard to do correctly

We started to notice that too many pop-ups break the rules.

1. Pop-up blockers

Advertisers started to misuse of pop-ups, breaking the rules of Expectation and Context.

Result? The "pop-up blocker"—at first a specific program and then feature built into popular browsers. And users don't like having to allow pop-ups.

2. Well-intentioned misuse of modes

Acrobat 5.0 came along. About one time in 10 it inexplicably locked up. After a while, we realized that this wasn't a defect; it was a "helpful feature." The dear little program was trying to help us by looking for a newer version of itself, but first, it popped up a window to ask whether we wanted it to do so. The dialog box is modal, so the program locks up while the dialog sits unanswered. Why is that a problem? Because too frequently it popped under instead of popping up, thus appearing to lock up Acrobat. This was a violation of the rule of Obvious Single Use.

3. Accessibility

Formal Investigation into Web Accessibility
http://www.equalityhumanrights.com/en/publicationsandresources/disability/pages/websiteaccessibilityguidance.aspx.

In 2004, the UK government commissioned a big report on web accessibility. One of its findings was specifically about pop-ups: "Until user agents allow users to turn off spawned windows, do not cause pop-ups or other windows to appear and do not change the current window without informing the user." Other authorities on accessibility said the same.

Why? Because disabled people are especially prone to violations of the rule of Knowledge. Let's think it through. Here's a disabled user who has fought way past a selection of links and focused attention on a small chunk of a complicated page. The user clicks... and, bingo, is expected to switch focus to some random point in another window:

- For a person using a screen magnifier, that new point may be off the screen.
- Someone who is dyslexic or has an attention disorder has to start all over again and reorient to a new window.
- A screen reader may not notice that the pop-up has appeared, so the screen reader user isn't informed that it is there.

And now, we all understand how important it is that our websites work just as well for people with disabilities as for all our other users. So we really can't recommend anything that might cause so many difficulties.

Farewell to pop-ups

Our current recommendation: The rules are broken too often for them to be useful. "Pop-ups: just say NO"...

...unless you are really sure that they will obey all five rules meticulously.

Part 3
Appearance

Taking Care of
the Details

7

The details of appearance

Up to now, we've been thinking mainly about the deeper aspects of the form: the relationship and conversation. Now it's time to concentrate on appearance—what it looks like.

We're going to start with eye-tracking evidence that shows the way that users look narrowly at the fields and labels when they are answering questions—and how that influences where you should place the labels. Then we'll continue to other details such as whether to put a colon at the end of each label and which font to use.

We'll think about larger issues in appearance, like branding, in the next chapter.

Don't stress over the details

Some of these details matter quite a bit to users. Others don't. But either way, our experience is that details can absorb a disproportionate amount of design time.

So we recommend this approach:

- Decide on one way to deal with each detail and then stick to it.
- Create a mini-style guide for your team or organization.
- Be flexible: allow changes to the style guide if there is real evidence that the changes will improve things for your users…
- … but not too flexible; otherwise, you'll end up with inconsistency between forms and even within forms. Users do notice consistency and value it.
- Avoid spending valuable design time arguing about the details.

Put labels where users will see them

When users first encounter a form, there are a whole lot of decisions going on. There are relationship issues ("Do I want to fill in this form?") conversation issues ("Are the questions appropriate?"), and appearance issues ("OK, where do I have to type?"). Where users look depends on which of these different issues is uppermost in their minds.

But once users are immersed in the conversation-for example, on the second page of a form that they expect to continue-they ignore everything other than the labels and fields.

We'll show you how this works with this page of a form from the Open University. On the previous page, the user has put in a postcode for the system to look up an address (a common way of dealing with addresses in the UK).

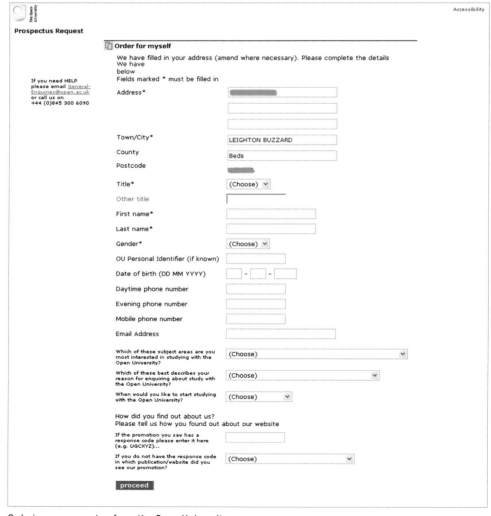

Ordering a prospectus from the Open University.

Eye-tracking shows that users focus narrowly on the fields and labels

Here is a heat map of the same page. You'll see that users focused narrowly on the labels and fields and barely looked at the rest of the form. They didn't need help, and they knew who published the form.

They skimmed rapidly over the top part of the form and then read more carefully when they got to the harder questions near the end.

Colored spots are places where users looked:
green is a glance;
yellow is looking longer;
red is where they looked the longest;
gray means that no one even glanced at it.
X is where someone clicked.

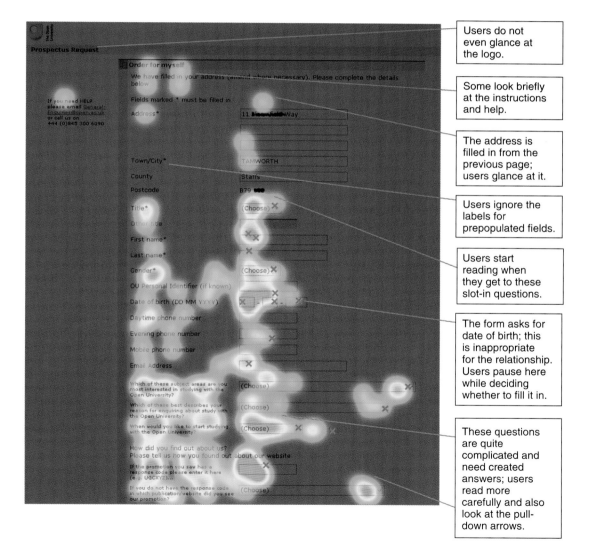

Users do not even glance at the logo.

Some look briefly at the instructions and help.

The address is filled in from the previous page; users glance at it.

Users ignore the labels for prepopulated fields.

Users start reading when they get to these slot-in questions.

The form asks for date of birth; this is inappropriate for the relationship. Users pause here while deciding whether to fill it in.

These questions are quite complicated and need created answers; users read more carefully and also look at the pull-down arrows.

A heat map of a form (ordering a prospectus from The Open University).

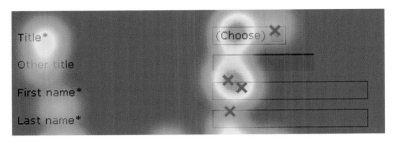

Detail from the heat map. Users focus closely on the left end of the fields.

One crucial point that we see in the heat map (and have observed in many, many usability tests) is that users focus closely on the left end of the fields. They barely, or never, even glance at the right end.

Users see labels above and to the left of fields

The label for the field can go in this area…

Or in this area to the left.

This area is invisible.

This area here is ambiguous.
Users may not see it at all until after they've filled in the field, or they may associate it with the next field.

Users look at labels for fields only if they think they are relevant

When we read, our eyes don't move smoothly. Instead, they jump and stop. Each jump is called a "saccade", and each stop is called a "fixation."

The address of the form is populated when the user first sees it. (We've grayed out his personal details).
He glances at it.

He skips the drop-down for "title." That will cause an error later.
The field has text in it and looks as if it might be pre-populated.

His eyes jump down to the first open entry field.

He glances across to its label ("Other title") but skips it.

He looks down for the next label with an asterisk.
It's "First Name," so he looks across to the empty box, types, and clicks.

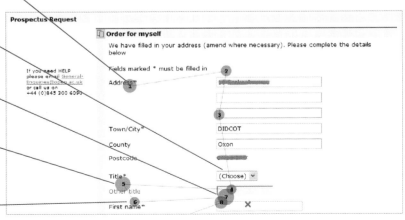

This eye track shows thin blue lines (saccades), large blue dots (fixations), and click (red "x") as a user works down the form.

This particular user didn't bother to read the instructions at the top of the form. He didn't look at the branding. He didn't need help. He saw only fields and labels: usually field first, then label, but not always.

Putting the labels above the fields works sometimes

In 2006, Mario Penzo did some eye-tracking experiments on where to place labels compared to fields. He measured the time of the saccades and found that the times are shortest when the labels are closest to the fields. That figures. If your eyes have to jump a shorter distance, they'll take less time to do it. Based on his research, Penzo recommended placing the labels above the fields.

Do you think that a shorter saccade makes a lot of difference to users when they're filling in forms?

Less eye movement is good, definitely. But it isn't the only design consideration.

For example, let's try it with the form we were using for eye tracking.

Label Placement in Forms
www.uxmatters.com/MT/
archives/000107.php

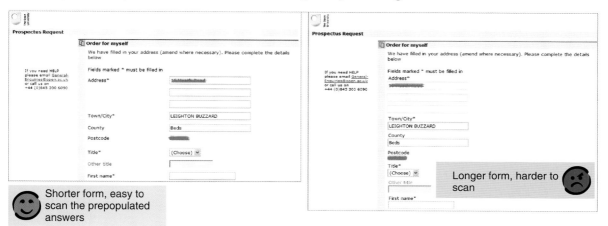

On the left, the original form. On the right, a version with labels above boxes.

In the example on the right, it's harder for the user to check the address. And the impression of a longer form offsets the benefits of shorter saccades.

There's also a deeper problem: for slot-in answers that users think of in groups (such as addresses), users are looking for the right slot for each bit of the answer in their heads. Putting the labels above the fields makes that harder.

If all your fields need slot-in answers, right-aligned labels can work well

There is a way to get shorter saccades and still make it easy for users to scan the labels: use right-aligned labels.

Short, simple labels work well for slot-in answers and also look good when right-aligned.

That's better: easier to read without the big gaps

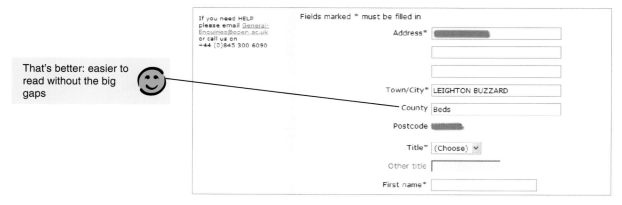

Another experimental version: this time, with right-aligned labels.

If all your fields need other types of answers, right-aligned labels are problematic

Other types of answers often need longer labels. Reading right-aligned text is harder, especially if your question runs over more than one line.

This gathered answer needs a longer label: not quite so good right-aligned.

This created answer needs a fully formed question. It's looking downright messy when right-aligned.

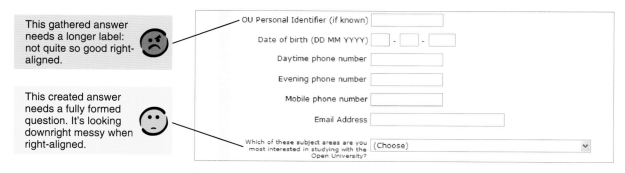

Further down the same experimental right-aligned form, there are some gathered and created answers. They need longer labels and don't work so well when right-aligned.

If your form asks for personal data, left-align the labels

Even if all your questions need slot-in answers, you need to think about the relationship before choosing the label alignment. If your users feel comfortable with revealing their answers, then they'll be speedily typing through the fields and right-aligning works.

But if the users are hesitating, they start to scan down the labels to assess how much they're being asked and how truthful they wish to be. Help them by left-aligning the labels to make them easy to scan.

If in doubt, left-align the labels

If you're sure that:

- users want to give you the information,
- all the questions require slot-in answers,
- the form is going to stay that way through revisions,

then right-align.

Otherwise, left-align and make it easier to read.

Special consideration: labels for translation

If your form will be translated, you need to think about how your design with adapt to the changing lengths of the labels, and the fields, if there are drop-downs. eBay's solution is to put all the labels above the fields so that when they expand and contract according to the different languages, the form design stays consistent.

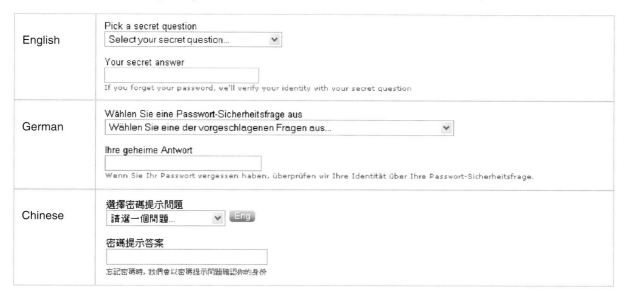

Questions from different versions of the eBay registration form.

But translating labels and drop-down text is probably one of the easiest parts of making your form available in another language. Chances are, you're also going to have to adapt it to the different cultural expectations of another country.

Here we go:

For example, look at these pieces from eBay forms for the United States, Germany, and Hong Kong. In each case, the user needs to input an address. It's not just the labels that change: it's the number of fields, the order of them, and what the fields ask for.

Address formatted for the United States	Street address ⬚ ⬚ City ⬚ State / Province [-Select- ▾] ZIP / Postal code [⬚] Country or region [United States ▾]
Address formatted for Germany	Straße und Hausnummer ⬚ *Bitte kein Postfach angeben* Ergänzende Angaben ⬚ Postleitzahl ⬚ Ort ⬚ Land oder Region [Deutschland ▾]
Address formatted for Hong Kong	國家或地區 Country or Region [香港 ▾] 住家地址 Address ⬚ ⬚

eBay changes the address format for different versions.

When you offer your form in a different language or to a different country, you are working with a whole new group of users and they have different expectations and needs. You'll need to revisit the work that you did when finding out about users the first place. And it's also extremely likely that your organization has also changed—that's the reason why you're adding another language, right?

All of these are likely to mean:
– new questions
– new topics
– a new flow through the topics
– and possibly, new branding or a new color scheme.

Changing the position of the labels is likely to be only a small part of the work that you have to do.

Make sure that each label is closely associated with its field

Finally, the really crucial point with labels and fields is that users associate the label correctly with the field that it goes with.

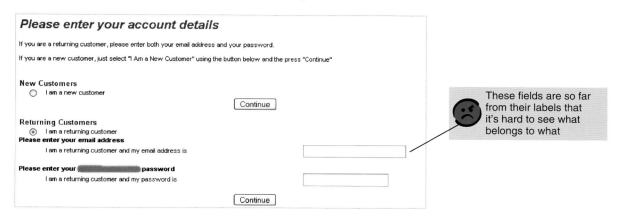

These fields are so far from their labels that it's hard to see what belongs to what

This form uses a completely liquid layout, so the fields wander away from their labels.

For people using screen readers, there's a simple solution: use the <label> element to tell the screen reader which label goes with which field.

But for everyone else, just choose a method of placement that makes sure you have an unambiguous close association—visually.

There are many good discussions online about how to achieve this placement technically. For example, http://www.alistapart.com/articles/practicalcss/

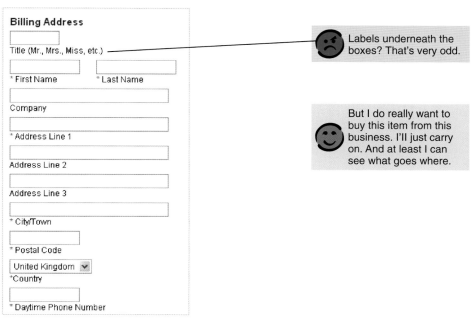

Labels underneath the boxes? That's very odd.

But I do really want to buy this item from this business. I'll just carry on. And at least I can see what goes where.

This form puts the labels in an unusual position, but we wanted to buy from this business, so we carried on with the form.

Colons at the end of labels?

Here's a detail that we have seen generate some especially lively debate among forms specialists, writers, and developers: whether or not to put a colon on the end of your labels.

The New York Times web forms have colons.   The *Times* (in London) does not.

At one time, screen readers had to rely on a variety of tricks for making sense of badly marked-up forms, so older accessibility checklists often insist on a colon.

But for web forms, if you mark up your form properly using the "label" tag, then the screen reader uses the markup to associate the labels with the corresponding fields so you don't need colons to help it.

Microsoft Vista guidelines for control labels: msdn2.microsoft. com/en-us/library/aa974176.aspx

The web address for the Apple guidelines is too long to include here. We found it by searching for: apple aqua guidelines text colon.

Microsoft Vista guidelines mandate colons; Apple Aqua is a bit more flexible. We think that's partly because screen readers have a harder time with desktops, which are directly displayed, compared to web markup, where they can read the source code. And it's partly for historic reasons: both Microsoft and Apple have lots of previous forms that had colons on the labels. Why go back to change them all?

We have tested a tremendous number of forms and never once has a user remarked on the presence or absence of colons. Even people who care about punctuation in other contexts don't seem to notice.

So if you want your web forms to be consistent with popular desktop environments, go with colons.

If you have lots of forms that use colons, go with colons.

If someone who matters to you has a strong opinion about it, go with that opinion.

Or just flip a coin. But stick to one method.

Right, that's enough of that. Let's try something that has more effect on users.

Sentence or title case for labels?

Our next detail is sentence case or title case: that is, whether to use capitals in labels as you would in a sentence, or Whether to Capitalize Every Word as in a Title.

The New York Times uses title case; the *Times* (of London) uses sentence case.

The New York Times uses title case.   The *Times* uses sentence case.

The eagle-eyed will have spotted that we chose sentence case for the headings in this book: we consider them to be more legible that way. And we prefer to use sentence case for our labels for the same reason.

But it's not a big deal: sentence case is only slightly more legible than title case.

The other argument against title case is one of interpretation: some designers apply it as in a proper title, where only the significant words are capitalized. But the easier, and quicker, option for programmers is to capitalize every word.

Sentence case:	Number we can use to contact you
Title case:	Number We Can Use to Contact You
Every word in capitals:	Number We Can Use To Contact You

The difference between title case and every word in capitals is minor, and we think that very few of your users will notice. But Opt For Every Word In Capitals And A Few Of Your Users Will Find Themselves Mentally Correcting Every "Wrongly" Capitalized Word. It's a bit like the use of apostrophes: most people don't notice whether or not you are "correct"; some people definitely do and their irritation about your "mistakes" will distract them from the smooth flow of questions and answers.

Our bottom line: opt for sentence case if you can. But if you have a big suite of forms that's all been done in title case, don't sweat it. Use your time on something that will give more benefits to your users, like learning what they do care about by doing some usability testing.

Indicating required fields

Now let's think about something that matters a little more again: required fields.

We have often seen people use required field indicators to assess the trustworthiness and effort of the form. They scan the form mainly to find out the level of invasiveness and, to a lesser extent, the amount of typing required.

What seems to be less important is exactly how you do the indicating.

Indicate required fields; if you want to indicate nonrequired, use "(optional)"

Most web forms use the convention of indicating required fields, rather than indicating optional fields. And most web forms use * (an asterisk) to indicate them. So, that's what users look for and what we recommend.

Approach	Comment	Verdict
Indicate required fields using * (an asterisk)	The most common method, therefore usually successful.	☺
Use a different indicator, such as "(required)" or a graphic	Works just fine; some extra benefit for people using screen readers (use the alt-text "Required field").	☺
Use the markup <required>	Works well for screen readers and therefore recommended. Use in addition to a visual indicator.	☺
Put the indicator near the label	It doesn't matter if the indicator is before the label, immediately after the label, or immediately before the field. Just pick one and be consistent.	☺
Indicate required fields by putting the label in a different color, e.g., red, as well as by having another indicator	Works well.	☺
Indicate optional fields by using "(optional)"	Works pretty well; works even better in addition to a required field indicator.	☺
Indicate required fields by putting the label in a different color e.g., red (but nothing else)	Doesn't work for people who are color-blind; may be misunderstood by some other users; no good for screen readers.	☹
Put the indicator on the right end of the field	Many users never see the right end of the fields, so this one will fail for them.	☹
Indicate optional fields (and leave required fields without an indicator)	Unusual, and therefore confusing.	☹

Include an explanation of the indicator you choose

Having a brief explanation of the required field indicator is helpful, so we put the explanation close to the top of the fields. Avoid hiding it in the preamble and definitely don't bother putting it at the end of the form. By then, it's too late.

An example: fussing with required fields

Here's a detail from a much longer form. We weren't happy with the required fields.

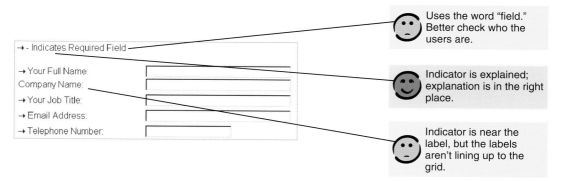

When we checked on our users, we found that they had no problem with the word "field." But we thought they might be unhappy about the labels not lining up neatly with the grid, so we asked the designer to move the labels nearer to the boxes.

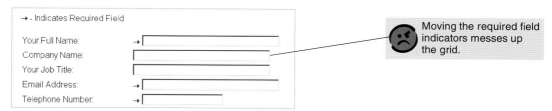

Now we have nice clear indicators, but unfortunately we have destroyed the grid. So we had a third attempt:

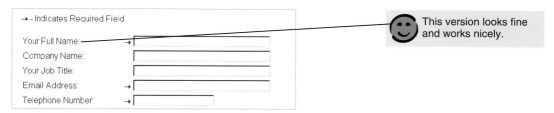

In the end, we got a tidy version, and it worked well for our users.

On reflection, the first version wasn't ideal, but it wasn't altogether bad. Maybe we could have used our time better by thinking about whether our users would be worried about giving us private data such as email addresses. In the end, what users really care about is the overall amount of work in the form, and we forgot about that in our fussing with details.

Choosing legible text: fonts and words

If you're using a nice big Verdana font for all the text on your forms and if your organization and users are happy with that, then you may want to skip this section.

But if you're getting into discussions about which font size to pick and why, here we go. We'll start with the basics and then look at some extra details.

Choose a good color contrast and large size of font

So far we've been putting black letters on a white background.

In Chapter 8, we recommend that you create a color sampler to show which color combinations from your site's color scheme are likely to be legible.

What happens when you want to be a bit more creative? Change the background, maybe? Use a fancier color than black? Exploit the overall site color scheme and branding in your form?

All these ideas are great. The trick is to make sure you have good contrast: the difference in color between the lettering and its background.

The higher the contrast, the easier it is to read.

For people with low vision, good contrast is crucial, closely followed by the option of setting their own contrast.

Some people with low vision find it easier to read light text on a dark background, like this.

A good font size is large enough to be read comfortably, but not so large that it is difficult to scan entire words or groups of words.

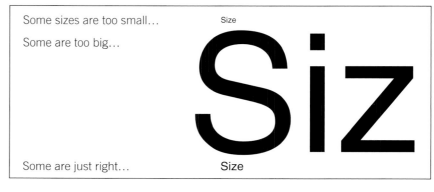

It's crucial to allow users to change their font size. Some people with low vision rely on being able to increase font sizes enormously. For most people, that small print gets more difficult to read each year after age 40. A polite site offers a "font size change" utility to make changing font size easy for its less web-savvy visitors. A really thoughtful site offers "display options" that allow users to change even more.

But it's even more important to pick a big enough size in the first place. Suppose you want to put some hints in a smaller size; in that case increase the main body text a size or two instead of shrinking the "small print."

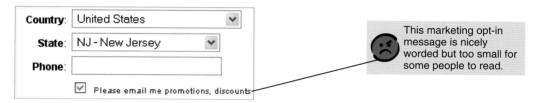

Detail from an e-commerce site: a polite opt-in message is spoiled by its tiny font.

Use typographic variations with restraint

You **MAY** be _tempted_ to use **bold**, _italic,_ and CAPITALS and <u>underlining</u> to emphasize **IMPORTANT INFORMATION**. Problem: you <u>can</u> END UP with a sort of _VISUAL SOUP_ where **none** of the **_emphasis works_**.

We used to see this sort of variation all the time on the web, especially in "thank-you" messages at the end of a process. These days, it seems to be mostly confined to instructions and terms and conditions. If you find yourself using ALL CAPITALS, think again.

This variation...	Is good for...	But causes problems for...
Bold	Scanning: words pop out of the context.	Continuous reading: the popped-out words disturb the reading pattern.
Italic	Emphasis in continuous reading	Scanning: the words don't pop out enough.
		Sloped shapes don't work well in low-pixel environments like computer screens.
ALL CAPITALS	Nothing, really. Possibly allowable if you need to refer your users to something elsewhere that is in all capitals.	Legibility: words in all capitals are less familiar and therefore harder to read.
<u>Underline</u>	Indicating links—and nothing else	Legibility: cuts across descenders in letters like "p" and "g."
		Consistency: users expect to be able to click on any underlined text.

Bold italic for emphasis here

CAPITALS for emphasis here

Bold for emphasis here. Why? Is all that variation meant to tell us something? Or is it accidental?

FINAL THOUGHTS [return to top]

Before you begin work on your application, please be aware of the following:

Don't wait until the last minute! (We can't emphasize that enough - things get busy right before deadlines, and you need to leave time for the "unexpected.") Early filing of the application forms also ensures your selected colleges have time to give your application thorough consideration and time to contact you, if necessary.

Check the list of application deadlines to ensure your selected colleges receive all parts of your application by their due dates. And be sure you know exactly what needs to be submitted in order for you to be considered for admission.

Each time you move from tab to tab, your information will NOT automatically be saved. To save your data, simply click on the Save button at the top or bottom of the screen.

In order to complete the online electronic submission process, be sure to logout of your application session upon viewing the final submission confirmation screen.

When you finish working and leave the online application, please be sure to log off. The log off button is located at the top of the screen and closes your application. Students who forget to log off risk security breaches. FOR YOUR SAFETY, IF THERE IS NO ACTIVITY WITH YOUR APPLICATION FOR 1 HOUR, YOU WILL AUTOMATICALLY BE LOGGED OFF.

If at any time you have any questions about the application process, feel free to contact the colleges directly. Addresses, phone/fax numbers, and e-mail addresses are available on this site. Go to app.commonapp.org, click on the College Info link, and find your college. The screen will display your selected college's contact information.

Our goal at the Common Application and ApplicationsOnline is to give you the best possible online experience with unsurpassed customer service. If you have any difficulty completing the online application, or have questions or comments, feel free to use the Help feature on the Welcome page, app.commonapp.org.

Mixing different typographic variations can result in a visual soup. This was a small section of the instructions for the Common Application, https://app.commonapp.org in March 2007.

This version looks well structured and is much more useful.

Pity that the contrast isn't good.

HELP

The 'Help' area provides you access to Frequently Asked Questions and other technical information that may be helpful while you are working on your application. If you still need assistance, the 'Help' area provides you with an online request form where you may seek assistance from our technical support team. The 'Help' link is located at the top right and bottom center of each page of the online application.

YOUR ACCOUNT

Make sure your email address is kept accurate so that you can receive important information about deadlines and other admissions information from the Common App or your selected institutions. Ensure that your email account will receive correspondence from caohelp@ayrecruiting.com by adding this to your safe list.

STARTING YOUR APPLICATION

You may start your application in either the My Colleges section by adding those institutions to which you wish to apply, or in the Bio section where you can start entering information about yourself.

Note that all required questions are indicated by a yellow dot.

A year later, the instructions were completely revised. They are orderly and much easier to read, both in content and typography. A section of the instructions for the Common Application, https://app.commonapp.org in March 2008.

Use white space to make easy-to-read paragraphs

If lines of text are too short, it's hard to form meaningful phrases. So they are hard to read.

If you have to use short lines, then breaking each line on a meaningful phrase makes them a little easier to read.

On the other hand, if lines are too long, they also become harder to read as your eyes have to jump back too far and can miscue. The effect is more striking as the font size becomes smaller, as we have tried to show you with this paragraph. We often see very long pages of terms and conditions where tiny fonts and long line lengths combine to make complex text even harder to read.

If lines are too long, you can compensate to some extent by increasing the white space between the lines. This space is known as the "leading." In this paragraph, we've increased the leading a little. If you do increase the leading within paragraphs, then make sure that you increase the gap between paragraphs even more.

If there is too little leading (like in this paragraph), lines become very crowded, and ascenders (such as in the letters "h" and "d") and descenders (in letters "p" and "q," for example) bump into the text on adjacent lines.

If there is too much leading, on the other hand (as there is in this paragraph), the lines of text look like they do not belong

together.

Summary: Taking Care of the Details

It's worth getting the details of your design right, but not worth arguing about them or fussing with them if there is more important work to be done.

If you want a set of details that works easily, then go with these suggestions:

If...	Place labels...	
Speed of reading the prompts is all-important and users will not need to scan the form before filling it in	Above the box	
In forms with all slot-in answers, where the users are happy about revealing the answers	Before the box, right justified	
In all other cases, or if you are unsure	Before the box, left justified	

- End each label with a colon.
- Use sentence case for labels.
- Use an asterisk as a required field indicator, supplemented by the <required> markup and a short explanation of the indicator at the start of the fields.
- Choose a legible font such as Verdana, use it at a large size, and make sure that users can easily change the size.
- Aim for a line length that is long enough to create coherent phrases but short enough to allow easy eye-movements back to the start of each line.

Serif or sans serif font?

We quite often get asked whether to use serif or sans serif fonts.

Serifs are the little extra decorative flourishes on some fonts.

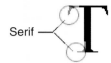

Serif

- This serif font is Times New Roman.
- This serif font is Palatino.
- **This sans serif font is Verdana.**
- This sans serif font is Arial.

Argument rages about whether serifs make text easier or more pleasant to read. We take the view that the main factor in the legibility of fonts is familiarity; that's why most of us can read our own handwriting more easily than other people can read it.

A great deal of legibility research was done in the 1950s and 1960s, when serif fonts were the standard and research was done on paper. So, serif fonts generally won because people were more used to reading them.

There is a good review of the literature on serif compared to sans serif at www.alexpoole.info/academic/literaturereview.html

Today, sans serif fonts are much more common, especially so on the Web. And they have some advantages. If a typical screen has 1280 pixels and is 19″ on the diagonal, then each horizontal inch has just over 86 pixels (the dots that make up the letters). Whereas most ordinary desktop printers have around 600 dots per inch, high-quality printing (like this book) runs at least 1200 dots per inch. This lack of dots means that serifs don't work well on screen.

On a printed page, the serifs are smooth, elegant curves.

On screen, the serifs are jagged.

These letters are both 36-point Times New Roman, enlarged.
On the left: from a book   On the right: on screen.

That's why Verdana was designed; it survives the low-pixel screen environment relatively well. It has a number of features that make it more legible than Times New Roman for the same point size when used as an on-screen font. We've picked out some of them here.

The "x-height" is the height of an "x", an ordinary letter without an ascender (the tall bit on an "h") or a descender (the lower bit of a "g"). Verdana has a large x-height compared to its overall size.

The stroke thickness in Verdana doesn't vary much, even in the "S".

The strokes in Times New Roman vary a lot in thickness. The subtle detail does not render well on screen.

Sample x-height Verdana
Sample x-height Times New Roman

The holes in the letters are "counters" (for example, in an "e"). Times New Roman has small counters for its size. The counters in Verdana are much more open.

We find typography fascinating. But we recognize that most of the time, it's just a matter of picking one standard font (usually Verdana) and using it at a large enough size.

Don't rule out other fonts though. Times New Roman works perfectly well in the newspapers it was designed for and can be fine if you use it at a large enough point size for its details to work. And there are plenty of other less common fonts that can enliven your pages. Used carefully, they can make the page more interesting and still be easy to read.

The Freakonomics site uses several different fonts to reflect the brand.

The quirky use of different fonts on the Freakonomics site reflects the personality of the book that it publicizes.

Making a Form
Look Easy

What makes a form look good

Your users will feel better about filling in your form if it looks easy.

> *If a Web site strikes me as beautiful, I will gladly give away my credit card number—is that how it goes?*
>
> *With our Swedish users, that is exactly what we experienced: users admitted to making intuitive, and rather emotional, on-the-spot decisions to trust a service provider when shopping online.*
>
> *A user comment included: "if it looks pleasant, I just trust it." (Karvonen, 2000)*

We love it when we have the luxury of working with graphic designers; making things look great comes naturally to them. But often we're on our own, so here are some things that help a form to "look pleasant":

- The form clearly shows who publishes it and what it is for.
- The form fits in with the overall branding of the site that owns it.
- You can easily escape into the rest of the site if you want to.
- The labels and fields line up neatly, both horizontally and vertically.
- It's visually grouped into topics.

And most important: all these things are done with restraint. Forms are rarely the best place to show off your creativity. Keep them looking simple.

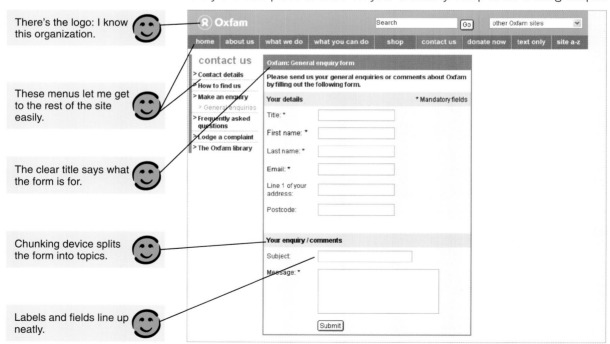

A good form fits with the site branding, looks orderly, and is simple.

Make sure users know who you are: logos and branding

Your users can arrive at your form from anywhere. It helps to create confidence if you show clearly who you are and provide routes into the rest of your site as well.

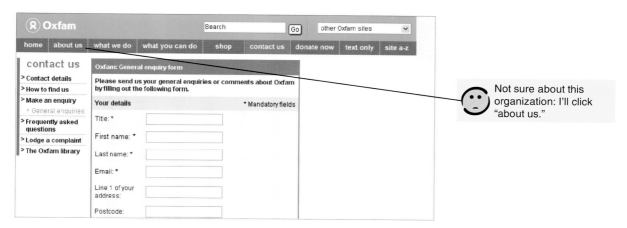

If you're not sure what "Oxfam" is, there's an easy way to find out.

On Oxfam's simple, blocky site, its strong use of color works equally well on the form and on other pages of the site, giving a strong sense of continuity.

Too little branding undermines confidence

If you don't continue your branding onto your form, it looks sloppy and undermines user confidence.

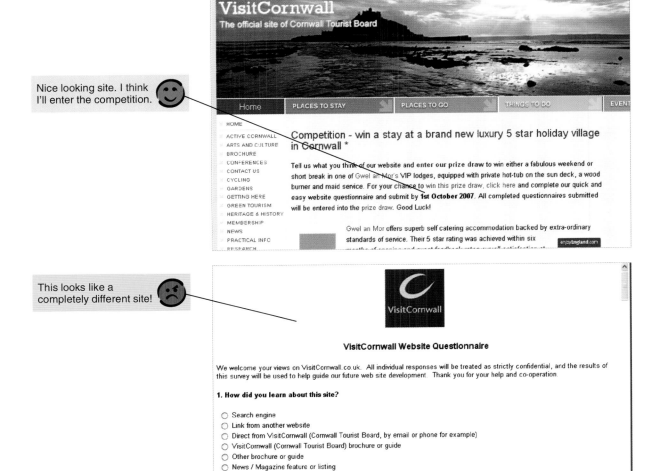

This site and its form are branded differently: not a good idea.

If you have to hand off to a third-party service that is branded differently, make sure that you warn your users about what will happen.

If we have to send users off to a third-party site, we've wondered about providing a thumbnail of the site to give a visual warning (as well as a written one). But we're not sure, as it might add to possible visual confusion, and we haven't found any examples.

What do you think?

Too much branding is almost as bad as too little

If you're working with brand elements that are very strong on the page, these elements can also cause problems when users arrive at the form.

Marvel Movies offered a sweepstake.

This branding certainly looks like the same site, but the sweepstake entry form is below the fold.

This thumbnail of the page shows how the branding dominates the form.

Take care with color combinations

Most designers can use black text on a white background in their forms—a great choice for legibility.

If your brand calls for something different, try making a test pattern. This will show if you're likely to hit legibility issues. We've made one for a bright blue, red, and yellow, and this color scheme makes it easy to see which combinations are going to fit the brand but be legible at the same time.

It's also a good idea to find some users who are color-impaired (for example, around 8% of men see some reds and greens as similar) and ask them about which combinations do and don't work for them.

Check out Juicy Studio's color contrast analyzer (juicystudio.com/services/colourcontrast.php)

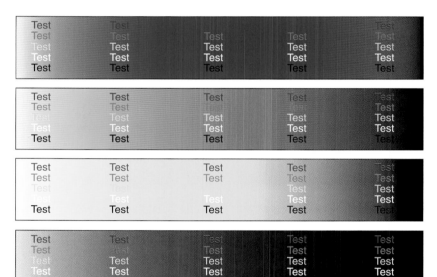

Creating a test pattern shows you which color combinations will work. This one looks for legibility when using bright red, blue, and yellow.

If you have to use a color combination that is marginal for legibility, try making the font larger and bolder. There's an example on the next page.

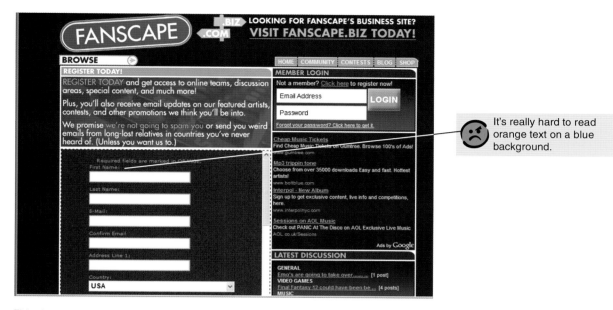

This site uses a bright blue and orange branding—a tough combination for legibility.

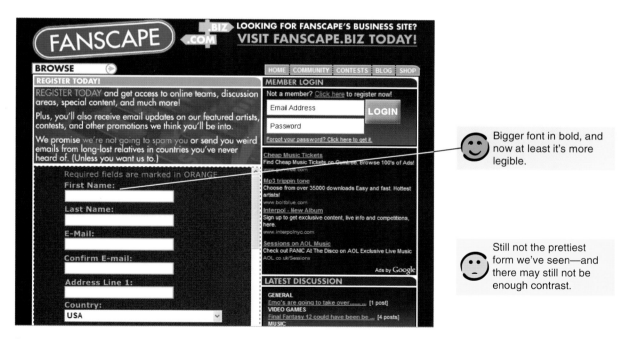

Our version uses a bigger size in bold to give it a better chance at legibility.

Use a light touch when applying branding to labels, fields, and buttons

A little creativity applied to the labels, fields, and buttons can help bring them into the overall look of your brand.

This form's fancy decorative detail echoes the old-fashioned look of the brand.

A little decoration on the buttons helps them to fit in with the brand, but they still look like buttons.

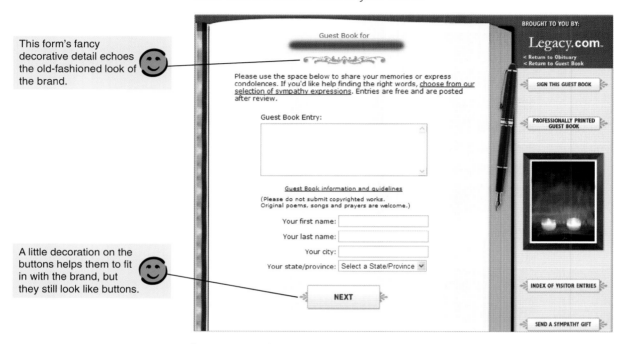

Legacy.com provides online memorial guest books. The company's brand mimics a formal paper book.

But in the end, it's up to the rest of your site to create a brand impression. By the time users get to the form, they just want to fill it in with the minimum of fuss. Don't confuse them with peculiar formatting.

Am I supposed to type into this form or print it and mail it?

This contact form has nonstandard data entry fields that fit the elegant look of Montblanc, a luxury brand, but confused users. It was changed to a standard form shortly after launch.

When users look at branding—and when they don't

Provided there is some continuity from the previous page, users barely notice the branding when they arrive at the form. And when they are immersed in the question-and-answer dialogue, they barely notice other elements on the screen. But when their task changes, then the rest of the page becomes very important.

For example, we tested the following page from a library search. Users wanted to find a book by Dan Brown, the best-selling author of *The Da Vinci Code*. They typed "Dan Brown," which gave no results. And they kept trying. It never worked.

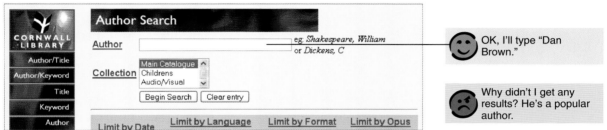

OK, I'll type "Dan Brown."

Why didn't I get any results? He's a popular author.

Users repeatedly ignored the hint about typing the author's surname first.

Like the users of the Open University form in the introduction, the users here focused narrowly on the labels and the parts of the fields that they were typing into while they were in the question-and-answer conversation.

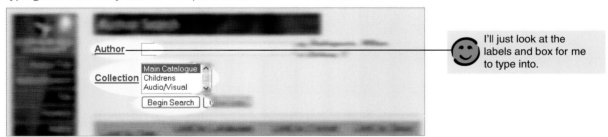

I'll just look at the labels and box for me to type into.

When users were immersed in questions, the rest of the form faded away.

But when they continued to get no results, they became frustrated. "Can I get help?" "Is there something else I can do?" They snapped out of the narrow focus and started to look at the rest of the form. That's when the branding and overall navigation really matters.

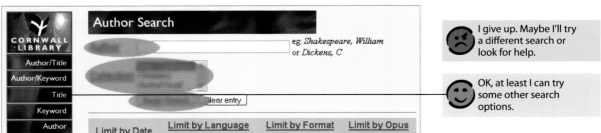

I give up. Maybe I'll try a different search or look for help.

OK, at least I can try some other search options.

When users changed task from answering questions, the rest of the page snapped into view.

Don't meddle with the user's browser

Some designers remove parts of the browser chrome because they want users to concentrate on their designed path through the form. The problem is that users may want to change task partway through: to get help, to check the privacy policy, to visit another website temporarily because someone interrupted them, and many other reasons.

So before you make changes to the browser, ask yourself these three questions:

- Are you confident that your form is more important than anything else the users might be doing at the same time?
- Are you sure that there are no unanticipated needs that users may have, such as looking up information elsewhere on their computer?
- Have you validated these views with observations of users in their own environment?

If the answer to all three questions is "yes," then maybe it is OK to remove parts of the browser.

If you're not sure about the answers, then possibly you need to do some more investigation or testing.

If any answer was "no" or "unsure," then don't meddle with the browser.

Make your form look tidy with grids

If your form lines up neatly, it will look tidy and professional. If it doesn't line up, it will look messy and amateurish.

Grids are ubiquitous in most media. Professional newspapers, magazines, brochures, and websites all use grids. A good grid gives structure and coherence to a form.

We can only touch lightly on the topic of grids here. See "Further Reading" for some of our favorites on grids.

Occasionally, we come across a form that fails to line up horizontally, usually because it wasn't tested in a variety of browsers.

This form lined up horizontally in Internet Explorer 5.

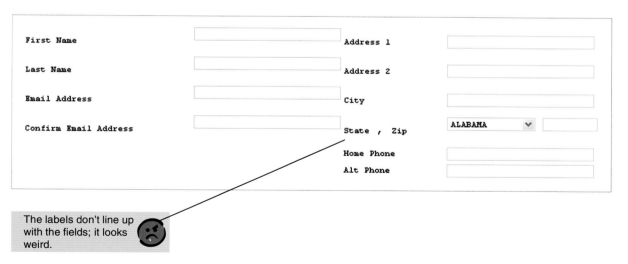

It looked like a complete mess in Firefox.

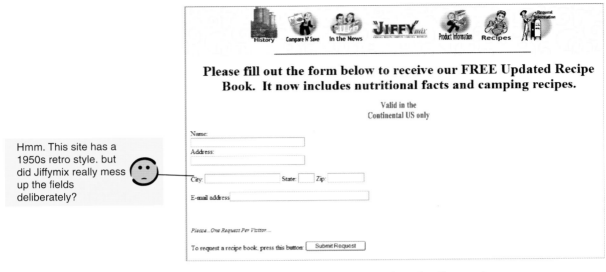

Hmm. This site has a 1950s retro style. but did Jiffymix really mess up the fields deliberately?

This Jiffymix form has a 1950s look, but is it intentionally messy?

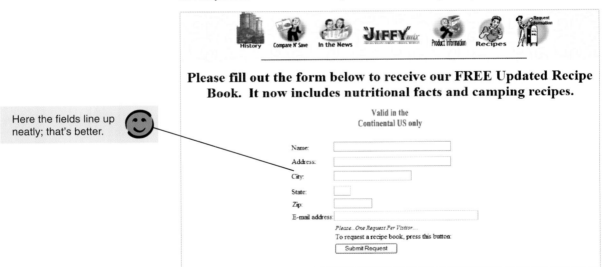

Here the fields line up neatly; that's better.

Our first redesign looks tidier (but still in keeping with the overall brand).

Line up to a few, strong vertical gridlines

Let's draw the vertical lines of the grid onto our example.

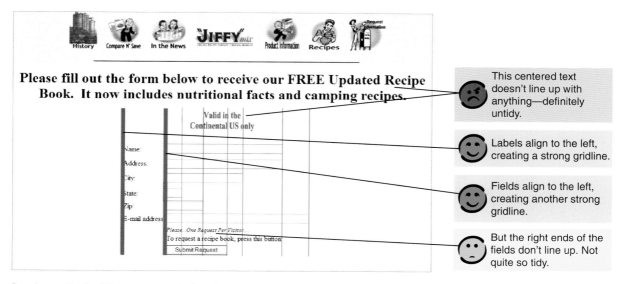

Drawing vertical gridlines on our redesign shows that we could do better.

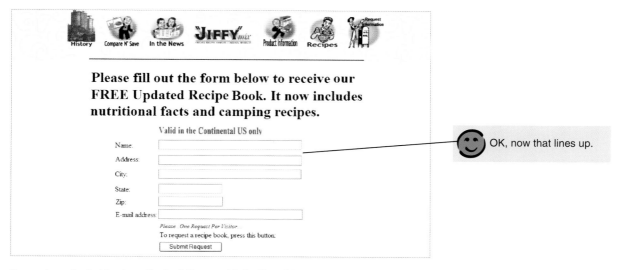

Now we've adjusted to six vertical gridlines and left-aligned text.

Do you think we overdid the tidiness on our example form?

Too few gridlines can look boxy; too many looks messy. The best solution is a compromise.

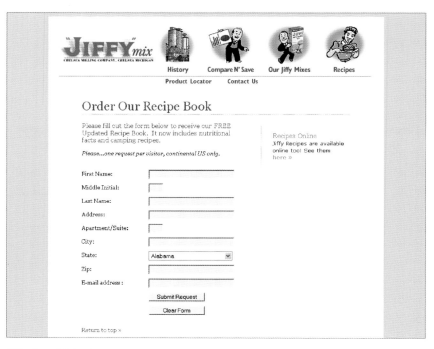

Jiffymix redid the form while we were writing this book.

We like the visual style of Jiffymix's new design, but not the way the "Name" question is split up or the "Clear Form" button.

What do you think?

Create a distinctly different gridline instead of failing to match an existing one

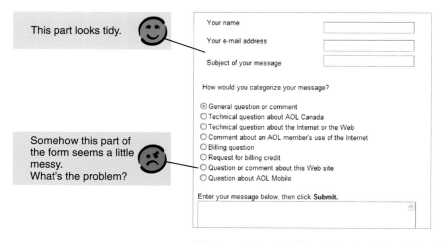

This part looks tidy.

Somehow this part of the form seems a little messy.
What's the problem?

This is part of an AOL Canada feedback form. It's quite orderly but somehow looks a little messy on the left.

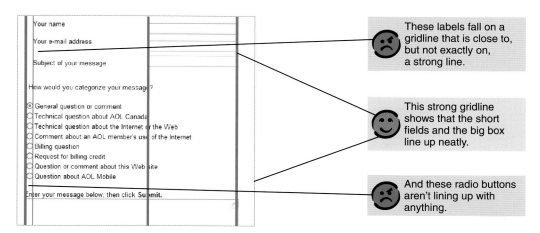

These labels fall on a gridline that is close to, but not exactly on, a strong line.

This strong gridline shows that the short fields and the big box line up neatly.

And these radio buttons aren't lining up with anything.

Drawing on some red gridlines shows that the labels and radio buttons don't quite line up.

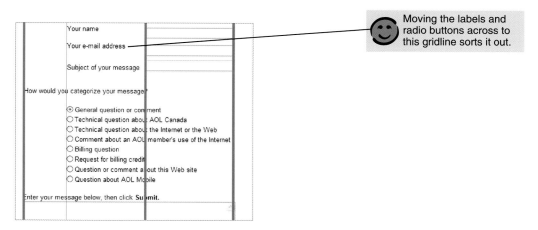

Moving the labels and radio buttons across to this gridline sorts it out.

Creating a definitely different gridline sorts out the problem. Everything now lines up neatly.

Make the form look organized with grouping

When you have long forms, grouping can help make the questions more manageable for the users.

For more details on <fieldset > , see http://www.webaim.org/ techniques/forms/screen_reader. php.

As with labels, grouping for people using screen readers is simple: use the <fieldset> markup element.

For everyone else, you have to make visual groups, as in the example. Even if you don't read German, you'll probably see two groups of fields.

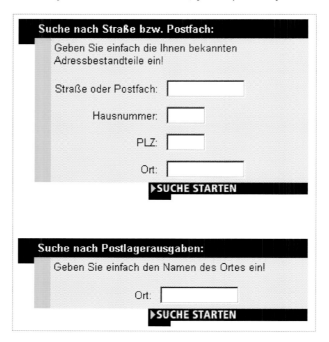

In this section from a German form, the five fields are clearly in one group of four and a second group of one on its own.

Ways of making groups	In our example
Placement	Four fields are close together; one is much further away.
Lines	The black lines above and below start and stop the groups; the yellow line to the side also aligns with the groups.
Backgrounds	The pale yellow background aligns with the groups.
Typography	White-on-black type announces the start and stop of each group; black-on-pale-yellow shows "within the group."

Placement is the easiest, clearest way of showing groups

Even small adjustments in placement can make a big difference in showing the structure of your form. Move things that go together a bit closer together; put things that don't go together a bit further apart.

Title: *	Title: *
First name: *	First name: *
Last name: *	Last name: *
Email: *	Email: *
Line 1 of your address:	Line 1 of your address:
Postcode:	Postcode:

These fields are OK, but the completely even spacing makes them look like one big block

Adjusting the placement slightly shows more clearly what goes with what, making it look a bit easier

A little adjustment of placement can also help to sort out ambiguities such as the problem with the radio buttons in the following example.

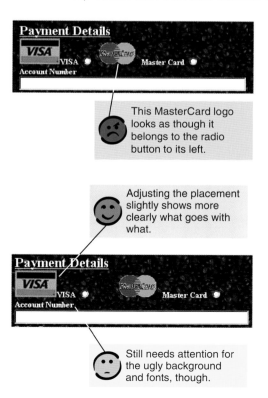

This MasterCard logo looks as though it belongs to the radio button to its left.

Adjusting the placement slightly shows more clearly what goes with what.

Still needs attention for the ugly background and fonts, though.

Lines may undermine grouping; try taking some out

We often see lots of lines on forms. Taking a few out can help.

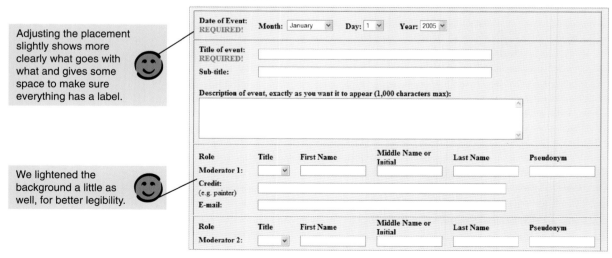

These lines don't work. Too many lines, not enough obvious groups.

These fields don't have any obvious labels

In this section from an event booking form, the lines seem to be trying to help associate labels and fields but are actually separating them.

Think about the purpose of each line:

- Is it meant to be separating one group from another? If so, leave it in.
- Is it dividing two things that ought to be grouped together? If so, take it out.

Adjusting the placement slightly shows more clearly what goes with what and gives some space to make sure everything has a label.

We lightened the background a little as well, for better legibility.

Our version adjusts the placement and makes sure all the fields have labels.

Don't break patterns

Humans rapidly learn and retain patterns, especially visual ones.

Once you have set a visual pattern, make sure that you don't break it later in the form.

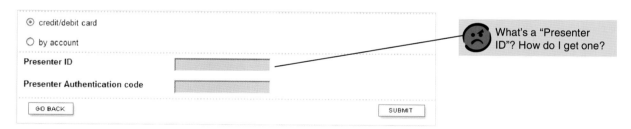

This step in one form uses a subtle dotted line to reinforce smaller groups and a solid line for larger groups.

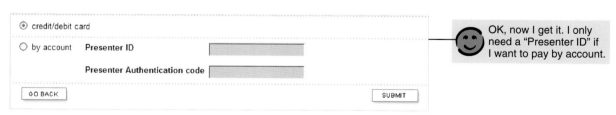

At another step, the same dotted line makes it look as though the user has to fill in "Presenter ID" and "Presenter Authentication Code" (our user didn't know what they were).

Our redesign moves the dotted line to conform to the previous pattern. Now it's obvious when you need "Presenter ID."

Don't hide content in grouping devices

Remember how people look either at the fields and labels, or at the rest of the page?

Your grouping devices (headings, dividing lines, shading, whatever) count as "the rest of the page." Users see them and see the way that they group fields together. But they don't read these devices while they are working on questions and answers.

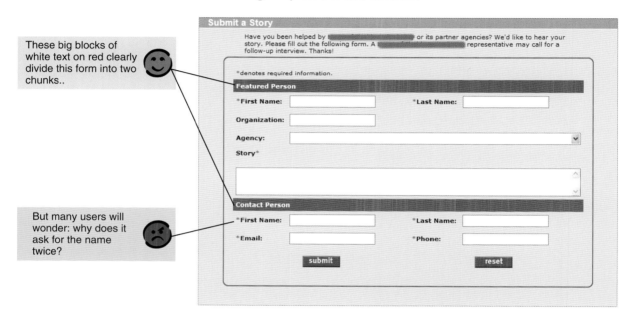

These big blocks of white text on red clearly divide this form into two chunks..

But many users will wonder: why does it ask for the name twice?

This form is divided visually into two clear groups. But many users filling it in will look only at the fields and labels, so they will think that the form asks for "First Name" and "Last Name" twice.

Here are some ways to solve the problem of content that is hidden in grouping devices:

1. Repeat the content outside the grouping device.
2. Move the content from the grouping device.
3. Rethink the questions altogether.

Following are examples of each of these approaches.

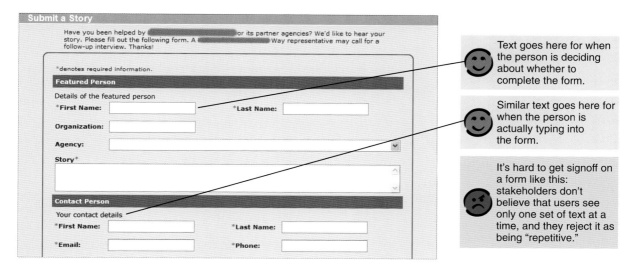

Quick fix: Repeat the content outside the grouping device.

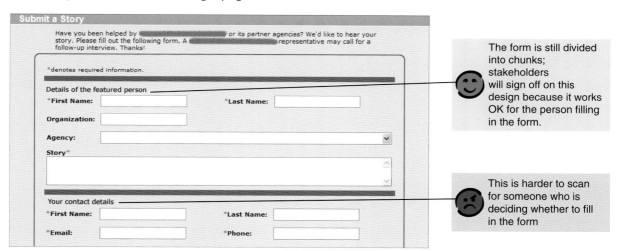

Another quick fix: Move the content from the grouping device.

Another way: Rethink the questions altogether.

Do you think "I could design a better form than any of those?"

If so, you're probably right. We just wanted to show that forms design is often a compromise between stakeholder needs, visual design, and user needs and behavior.

Avoid two-column forms

We're pleased to see that there are fewer and fewer examples of two-column layouts. At first glance, these layouts seem like a good idea; they offer users more options in a smaller amount of screen space.

Login

Don't have an account yet?

In order to serve you best, please proceed to create an account now.

First Name* : [   ]

Last Name*: [   ]

Email*: [   ]

Password*: [   ]

All fields are required.

[Create an Account]

Existing Customers:

Welcome back

Email: [   ]

Password: [   ]

[Log In]

Forgot your password? Click here

Typical two-column login form: the user is meant to choose the left column or the right column.

The problem is that users don't look at the form as a whole; they focus narrowly on the first box to type into.

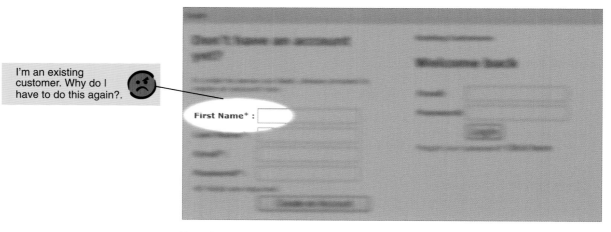

Users focus narrowly on the first box to type into.

On a typical logon form, the problem is only momentary: the user quickly snaps out of the question-and-answer conversation, looks at the form as a whole, and sees the "existing customers" column. And the user has now learned the grouping pattern: "Two columns mean choice—either left column or right column."

But we also see two-column layouts that mean "go down the left column and then go down the right column" or "go across left to right and then go down." These are some examples on the next page.

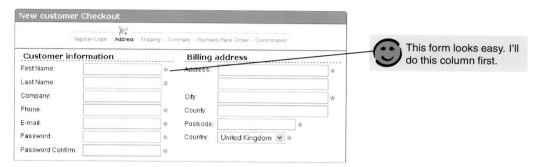

This form is arranged in two columns and is meant to be filled down the left column and then down the right column.

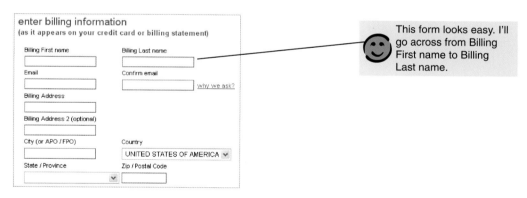

This part of a form is arranged in two columns and is meant to be filled from left to right, row by row.

Both of the preceding examples are OK. But we had to look hard for them. What we see more often is two-column forms that have misleading reading orders—ones that look as though they should be filled left column and then right column, but in fact you have to go across. Or vice versa.

It looks as though I'm supposed to fill in the left column first. So why is "Given name" on the right?

"Frequent Flyer Programme" should be grouped with "Frequent Flyer Number," but they are in separate columns.

This form looks as though it should be filled left-column and then right column, but in fact it is meant to be filled in across and then down.

And sometimes we see arrangements that mix reading orders.

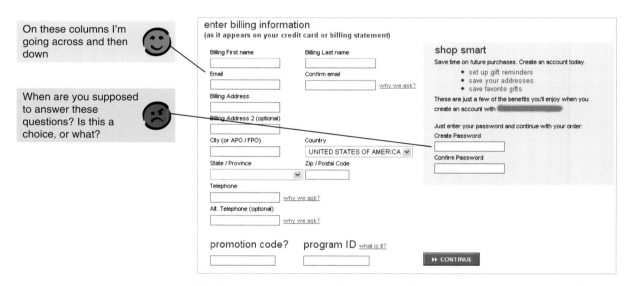

On these columns I'm going across and then down

When are you supposed to answer these questions? Is this a choice, or what?

This form starts as across and then down, but then changes to down the left and down the right.

If you are trying to cram a lot of fields onto a page, then stop to think about the reading order. Remember the narrow focus. We usually find that a bit of scrolling is much better than two-column layouts.

Plotting the reading order on your form can reveal issues. That nasty upward jag after "program ID" doesn't look good.

Summary: Making a form look easy

When users are dealing with the questions and answers, they focus tightly on the fields and labels.

But when they swap to a different task, such as asking "Who are you" or looking for contact details, they snap out of the narrow focus and start looking at the page furniture. Help them by making sure your form is lightly but clearly branded as part of your site.

Lining up forms to a vertical grid makes them look tidy and thoughtfully designed; that increases user confidence in the form.

Forms look easier to handle if the fields are organized into groups. Placement is the easiest, clearest way of showing groups, but lines may undermine grouping.

Once you have established a grouping pattern, don't break it.

Two-column layouts can create ambiguous reading orders; users can go across horizontally or down vertically. Avoid using two columns.

The sample form in this case study is used by scientists who are collecting data about natural phenomena. The Organization of Biological Field Stations (OBFS) maintains a Data Registry that describes these data sets so that other scientists can find them and use them.

The original form asked questions that are reasonably easy to answer if you are a research scientist with a data set. But its organization and layout were confusing. It didn't flow well or look all that good, and it had several accessibility problems.

The actions

The form got a makeover:

- Used color/shading to make the topic groups clearer;
- Lightened background to improve readability;
- Reduced clutter and improved flow by grouping, aligning, and spacing elements appropriately. Cut out unnecessary words;
- Lined up the boxes to a grid to make it look more organized and easier to fill in;
- Moved labels to the left of data entry fields;
- Removed red text for required fields and replaced with standard asterisk symbol;
- Changed link style from green text to standard blue underlined;
- Made major sections expandable/collapsible to allow users to concentrate on different sections depending on their needs.

The result

Laura Downey, who did the redesign, said "OBFS now has a form that is easy to follow and fill out, and is well organized and looks good. The principals were happy with the redesign."

We'd like to thank Laura Downey, the University of New Mexico, and the Scientific Environment for Ecological Knowledge (SEEK) project for allowing us to use this case study.

Before—problematic

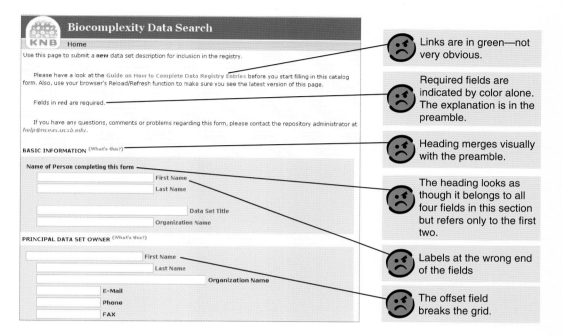

Biocomplexity Data Search
KNB   Home

Use this page to submit a **new** data set description for inclusion in the registry.

Please have a look at the Guide on How to Complete Data Registry Entries before you start filling in this catalog form. Also, use your browser's Reload/Refresh function to make sure you see the latest version of this page.

Fields in red are required.

If you have any questions, comments or problems regarding this form, please contact the repository administrator at help@nceas.ucsb.edu.

BASIC INFORMATION (What's this?)

Name of Person completing this form

First Name
Last Name

Data Set Title
Organization Name

PRINCIPAL DATA SET OWNER (What's this?)

First Name
Last Name
Organization Name
E-Mail
Phone
FAX

- Links are in green—not very obvious.
- Required fields are indicated by color alone. The explanation is in the preamble.
- Heading merges visually with the preamble.
- The heading looks as though it belongs to all four fields in this section but refers only to the first two.
- Labels at the wrong end of the fields
- The offset field breaks the grid.

After—successful makeover

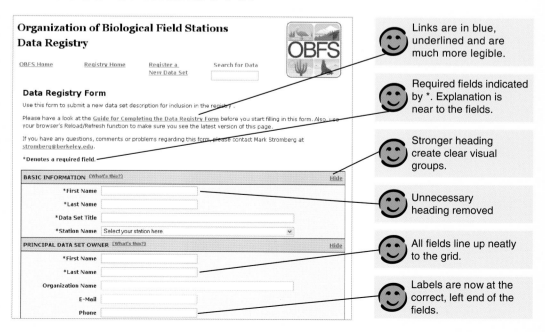

Organization of Biological Field Stations
Data Registry

OBFS Home   Registry Home   Register a   Search for Data
                                      New Data Set

Data Registry Form

Use this form to submit a new data set description for inclusion in the registry.

Please have a look at the Guide for Completing the Data Registry Form before you start filling in this form. Also, use your browser's Reload/Refresh function to make sure you see the latest version of this page.

If you have any questions, comments or problems regarding this form, please contact Mark Stromberg at stromberg@berkeley.edu.

*Denotes a required field.

BASIC INFORMATION (What's this?)   Hide

*First Name
*Last Name
*Data Set Title
*Station Name   Select your station here

PRINCIPAL DATA SET OWNER (What's this?)   Hide

*First Name
*Last Name
Organization Name
E-Mail
Phone

- Links are in blue, underlined and are much more legible.
- Required fields indicated by *. Explanation is near to the fields.
- Stronger heading create clear visual groups.
- Unnecessary heading removed
- All fields line up neatly to the grid.
- Labels are now at the correct, left end of the fields.

Part 4
Testing

Testing
(The Best Bit)

We're passionate about usability testing

If we could make one chapter in this book compulsory, it would be this one. The reason is that, despite our combined 30 years' experience with forms, we're still passionate about usability testing. We love it, it's fun, and most of all, it's the best way to find out what the problems might be on your forms.

Usability testing is easy and gets quick results

Usability testing is quick, easy, and inexpensive, and you *will* identify problems with your form. Some of them may be things that you suspected might be problematic, whereas others may take you completely by surprise.

There are many books and online resources providing excellent advice on usability testing. We've put some suggestions in "Further Reading."

At a minimum, you can conduct what we call a "hey you" test. Just get whoever is available to fill in the form, observing their actions and noting the issues that arise. The earlier, the better. This testing gives you more chance to do something about the problems you find, and users often feel more able to comment freely on something that's a bit rough-and-ready.

Usability testing an early paper prototype of a form. The designer is on the right taking notes. The user is on the left.

How we do expert reviews of forms

For a more formal version of this expert review process, see Jarrett and Quesenbery (2006).

Sometimes clients won't let us usability test forms. They say, "You're the experts. Tell us what you think." If that happens, we draw up a persona and then try our very best to "be" that persona as we fill in the form. We find a lot of problems, but we're always nervous about it—because we're *not* typical users. We're much too interested in forms, for a start. The same probably applies to you.

How to do really good usability testing of forms

While the "hey you" test has the benefit of being very easy to organize, it's likely that by testing with only one person, you'll miss some of the problems in the form.

Test with more users (five is usually enough)

We find that testing with five users is enough (one at a time, because most people fill in forms on their own). We usually plan for a couple of extras, to allow for people who don't turn up for whatever reason.

Clients sometimes don't believe us and force us to test with more people. It's OK, we're being paid, and we find out a little more from each extra user. But not much more: our experience usually mirrors the following graph. It shows that you uncover more problems with each additional user, but that the first few are the ones that really give you most information.

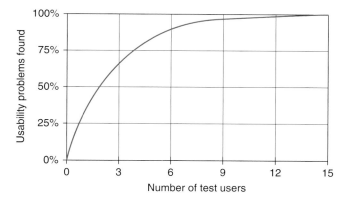

This graph comes from Nielsen and Landauer (1993).

We also find that it gets increasingly difficult to be genuinely interested in the 10th person who mostly tells you things you've heard several times already. So we try to persuade clients to start with five participants and then decide whether more tests are necessary (perhaps after a further round of design).

Try to get "real" users

Testing with the people who will actually complete your forms is by far the best. Failing that, you should try to get people as similar as possible to those users. You may have access to them directly, or you may be able to get an agency to organize them. We sometimes use market research recruiters; they typically have a large database of people and can match our required profile.

Think about how the participants you got are different from your target users

Whether you test with one participant or a dozen, you still need to think about how those participants are different from your target users.

There's always at least a little bit of difference. For one thing, they've agreed to spend part of their valuable time working on your form. So compared to your target users, were your participants

- More or less motivated?
- More or less knowledgeable about the topics in your form?
- More or less comfortable with the Internet and technology?

... and so on, looking at all the topics that make up relationship.

Then think about whether those differences may have affected their reactions to your form. We usually take the view that if a participant finds any problem, then we should take that response pretty seriously and probably do something about it. But if our participants don't find any problems, then we worry a lot more about whether they are different from our target users.

Think about where the users will find the answers

If your form has only slot-in and created answers, then it's quite OK to ask participants to complete it with the information in their heads. Make sure you will handle any personal information with appropriate care and give participants enough time to construct realistic created answers.

If your form has gathered or third-party answers, it gets a bit more complicated. Here are our ideas for providing the information they need when completing the form:

The approach	What you do	Risks and benefits
Have users provide the information	You can ask users to use real information from their own circumstances.	Can hit some problems if there are gathered or third-party answers and may hit privacy errors if the slot-in answers are too personal.
Provide an example	Write a brief story in everyday language that has all the gathered and third-party answers.	The easiest for you, but be careful to write a proper story, not just a list of answers in the same order as the form. There's no point in merely watching users copy answers from the example to the form.
Run a two-part test	Users come to you to do as much of the form as they can, then go away to get answers on their own and then return to debrief.	Realistic and less time-consuming for you than going to the users, but you're not really sure what happens when the users go away to find the answers, and this approach is also difficult to organize because users may drop out from the second part of the test.
Take the test to the users	Go to places where the users are. They find their own answers.	Most realistic and interesting. More time-consuming and may hit issues of privacy or confidentiality. Can also be awkward if you want to record the test sessions. Try to overcome the difficulties, because this is a wonderful way to test your form.

What's happening in the participants' heads?

When you watch people complete forms, it can be difficult to know what's going on and why they are doing particular things.

For example, we tested a form for job seekers. This form included an "Employer Search" button that looked for an employer for you. Job seekers ignored it. Because they didn't see it? Because they didn't want to use it? Or because they didn't know what it meant? We couldn't tell by watching. So we asked them. And it turned out that they saw the button but thought it meant a special search for employers to use.

The easy solution to this problem is to ask participants to "think aloud." You'll learn a lot more, even though talking their way through the form slows down the users a bit.

The snag is that some participants just don't do it. They say they will, but thinking aloud doesn't come naturally to them. Some participants start off thinking aloud very happily; then they hit a more complex bit of the form and go quiet—at the point when you really want those insights.

So we usually chat with users as they fill in the form, drawing on questions like these.

To find out whether the form is...	Ask questions like:
Meaningful	*Could you tell me what that question is asking you?* *What sort of information do you think that question is asking for?*
Relevant	*Did you expect to be asked that question?* *Does it explain why it asked that question?* *Did it leave out a question you expected?*
Easy or difficult	*How would you work out the answer to that question?* *Where would you look for the answer to that question?*
Asking appropriate questions	*Is it OK for the company to ask that question?* *Is that the sort of information you'd be willing to provide?*

Keep in mind that a usability test is not an interrogation. Be gentle, and if in doubt, allow users to proceed uninterrupted at their own pace. You'll still find out lots of interesting things.

Final message from this book

We wrote this book because we wanted to help you design great forms. We thought a lot about forms, asked many friends about their ideas and their experiences with forms, and read a lot of other books.

But in the end, we mostly found that what really matters is what we learned from observing users and looking at forms.

If you want to create great forms, usability test early and often

In the end, creating great forms is all about what users told us: the mistakes they made on forms. How they challenged us to create better forms. How they helped us to come up with the ideas and processes that we put in this book. And what they showed us when they tried the forms in tests and we learned what really worked for them.

Most of all, that's what we continue to do: test early and test often.

Form, document and questionnaire design in general

Forms design

Barnett, R. B. (2005) *Forms for people: Designing forms that people can use* ACT. Australia: Robert Barnett and Associates Pty Ltd.

> A comprehensive book that comes from Rob's many years of experience in designing paper forms. The 2005 edition includes many updates for electronic forms.

Wroblewski, L. (2008) *Web Form Design: Filling in the Blanks*. Brooklyn, New York: Rosenfeld Media

> Luke's excellent short book is practical and full of examples.

Beaumont, A., James, J., Stephens, J., and Ullman, C. (2002) *Usable Forms for the Web* Birmingham. UK: glasshaus Ltd.

> Primarily a book about building forms, and is now a bit out of date. Includes a good chapter on basic usability of forms and an equally good chapter on validations.

Reference books for forms terminology

Barnett, R. B. (1994) *The Form Designer's Quick Reference Guide*, 2nd ed. Belconnen. ACT Australia: Robert Barnett and Associates Pty Ltd.

> A comprehensive reference arranged alphabetically. Primarily describes paper forms, using plenty of short essays and illustrations. Intended for Australian readers but useful for anyone designing paper forms.

Green, M., Jarvis, B. M., McGarry, D. J., and Gerhard, R. A. (1990) *The Business Forms Handbook*. Alexandria, VA: National Business Forms Association.

> Similar to Rob Barnett's book but four times the size (and weight). Essential if you are printing thousands of different types of paper forms. For most of us, Barnett's book is enough.

Document design in general

Zwaga, H. J. G., Boersema, T., and Hoonhout, H. (1999) *Visual Information for Everyday Use: Design and Research Perspectives*. London: Taylor and Francis.

> Interesting collection of essays on information design, including three specifically on forms. Very readable for an academic book, with plenty of bibliography if you want to pursue references.

Schriver, K. A. (1997) *Dynamics in Document Design*. New York: John Wiley and Sons, Inc.

> Fascinating book on document design, with particularly strong chapters on "seeing the text" (typography and use of space) and "the interplay of words and pictures" (how graphics and text interact).

Hartley, J. (1994) *Designing Instructional Text*, 3rd ed. London: Kogan Page.

> Short, clear, and authoritative book on designing "instructional text." Aimed at teaching materials, but the advice works equally well on any text that is intended to convey information: Now out of print but generally easy to find (and worth the effort).

Questionnaire design

Dillman, D. A. (2007) *Mail and Internet Surveys: The Tailored Design Method*. New York: John Wiley & Sons Inc.

> When you pick up this book, don't be put off by its somewhat boring appearance and large size. It is packed with straightforward, realistic and helpful advice—backed by top-quality research. The 2007 edition contains interesting extra chapters including an analysis of the infamous 2000 "Butterfly Ballot" that had a pivotal effect in that year's US Presidential election.

Oppenheim, A. N. (1992) *Questionnaire Design, Interviewing and Attitude Measurement*. London: Pinter Publishers Ltd.

> Another book on questionnaire design that looks unattractive but is full of excellent advice.

Usability and accessibility in general

Books on usability in general

Krug, S. (2005) *Don't Make Me Think: A Common Sense Approach to Web Usability*. Indianapolis: New Riders.

> Accurate, enjoyable, short—the must-read book on usability for you, your boss and your friends.

Gaffney, G., and Szuc, D. (2006) *The Usability Kit:* Melbourne. Australia: SitePoint.

> Step-by-step kit for designing usable web sites with loads of blueprints offering practical solutions and patterns for blogs, product pages, shopping carts, and sitemaps.

Stone, D., Jarrett, C., Woodroffe, M., and Minocha, S. (2005) *User Interface Design and Evaluation*. San Francisco: Morgan Kaufmann.

> A textbook that is aimed at people who want to learn about user interface design from scratch on their own. Hardly anything in it about forms but the chapters on 'Persuasion' are relevant if you are having difficulty in getting your organization to support your usability efforts.

Online materials on usability in general

> The authoritative site on usability in general, with particular relevance to government and not-for-profit websites is
>
> www.usability.gov
>
> The Usability Professionals' Association is developing a Body of Knowledge for usability at:
>
> http://www.usabilitybok.org/

Resources for accessibility

Horton, S. (2005) *Access by Design: A Guide to Universal Usability for Web Designers.* Indianapolis: New Riders

Readable, clear, short book that explains how designing for people with disabilities helps everyone. Has a useful chapter on markup of forms. Also available as an online book at: universalusability.com

The UK Royal National Institute of Blind People has a good selection of pages on making information accessible:

http://www.rnib.org.uk/xpedio/groups/public/documents/code/public_rnib003460.hcsp

The World Wide Web consortium has a Web Accessibility Initiative. Home page and guidelines are at:

http://www.w3.org/WAI/

UK government website about the Disability Discrimination Act and how to comply with it:

http://www.direct.gov.uk/en/DisabledPeople/RightsAndObligations/DisabilityRights/DG_4001068

U.S. government website about Section 508, the law that mandates federal government to be accessible:

http://www.section508.gov/

The United Nations is working for the rights and dignities of disabled persons:

http://www.un.org/disabilities/

Finidng out how users work with forms

Relationship

Finding out about your users and your organization

Gerry Gaffney's site has downloadable, easy instructions on how to do investigation activities such as contextual inquiry and card sorting.

http://www.infodesign.com.au/usabilityresources

Henry, S. L. (2007). *Just Ask: Integrating Accessibility Throughout Design.* www.uiAccess.com

Short, clear book that explains how to involve people with disabilities throughout your project, particularly in the early stages. Also available as an online book at http://www.uiaccess.com/JustAsk/

Hackos, J. T., and Redish, J. C. (1998) *User and Task Analysis for Interface Design.* New York: John Wiley and Sons, Inc.

Although this book is over 10 years old, it is still the best book on why you should do site visits, how to do them, and what to do with your findings. Clear and practical.

Courage, C., and Baxter, K. (2005) *Understanding Your Users: A practical guide to user requirements*. San Francisco: Morgan Kaufmann Publishers, Inc.

> This hefty book (781 pages) is a comprehensive 'how to' manual that will take you step by step through a range of ways of finding out about your users and then turning that understanding into specific requirements.

Beyer, H., and Holtzblatt, K. (1998) *Contextual Design: Defining Customer-Centred Systems*. San Francisco: Morgan Kaufmann Publishers, Inc.

> A key resource on finding out about how users do their work. Quite difficult, but definitely worth the effort if you are working on a big project in a complex organization.

Pruitt, J., and Adlin, T. (2006) *The Persona Lifecycle: Keeping People in Mind Throughout Product Design*. San Francisco: Morgan Kaufmann Publishers, Inc,

> If your organization decides to commit to using personas as an ongoing way of understanding and thinking about your users, then you'll definitely need this large and thorough book.

Designing persuasive systems

Fogg, B. J. (2003) *Persuasive Technology: Using Computers to Change What We Think and Do*. San Francisco: Morgan Kaufmann Publishers, Inc.

> This challenging and thoughtful book draws extensively on work done at Stanford University on web credibility.

Conversation: making questions easy to answer

Questions and answers

Books on survey methodology are good sources of ideas about the design of questions and how people answer questions.

Tourangeau, R., Rips, L. J., and Rasinski, K. (2000) *The Psychology of Survey Response*. New York: Cambridge University Press.

Written for cognitive psychologists and survey methodologists, and backed by comprehensive references to the relevant research. We found this book helpful in working out our ideas on how users answer questions.

Sudman, S., Bradburn, N. M., and Schwartz, N. (1996) *Thinking about Answers: The Application of Cognitive Processes to Survey Methodology*. San Francisco: Jossey-Bass Publishers.

Not the easiest book to read, but worth the effort if it is important for you to get accurate answers to questionnaires.

Tanur, J. M. (Ed.) (1992) *Questions about Questions: Inquiries into the Cognitive Bases of Surveys*. New York: Russell Sage Foundation.

A convenient collection of chapters about research on questions. We particularly like the chapter by Suchman and Jordan, which describes in detail some horrible mismatches of questions being asked and questions being answered.

Choosing controls and other interface elements

Tidwell, J. (2006) *Designing Interfaces: Patterns for Effective Interaction Design*. Sebastopol, California: O'Reilly

Looks at a whole range of different patterns: the basic set of controls that we discuss in this book, and many other more complex ones. Has a good chapter on forms design.

Johnson, J. (2007) *GUI Bloopers 2.0: Common User Interface Design Don'ts and Dos*. San Francisco: Morgan Kaufmann Publishers.

Jeff Johnson has updated his popular book that is full of practical advice put across in a fun way.

Johnson, J. (2003) *Web Bloopers: 60 Common Web Design Mistakes and How to Avoid Them*. San Francisco: Morgan Kaufmann Publishers.

> Similar to GUI Bloopers, but focusing on the web.

37 signals (2004) *Defensive Design for the Web: How to Improve Error Messages, Help, Forms, and Other Crisis Points*. Indianapolis: New Riders.

> Short book with plentiful examples and practical tips.

Writing instructions

Redish, J. (Ginny) (2007) *Letting Go of the Words: Writing Web Content that Works*. San Francisco: Morgan Kaufmann Publishers.

> Wonderful book on how to structure content-rich web sites, and how to write for them. Beautifully written, very practical. If you only buy one book, make it this one.

Cutts, M. (1995) *The Plain English Guide*. Oxford: Oxford University Press.

> Small, thorough, and clear book on writing Plain English. Includes a short section on forms.

Gentle, R. (2002) *Business Writing That Works*. London: Pearson Education.

> A crisp set of guidelines on writing well, illustrated with before- and after- examples. Even shorter versions are available as training materials from: http://www.plainwriting.co.za/Training_material.htm

Readability tests

Balanced assessment of the value of readability tests:

http://www.plainlanguagenetwork.org/stephens/index.html

Please note: These tests have *some* value for continuous prose, as you will see if you read this article. However, they are almost completely useless for forms and questionnaires. The reason we say "almost completely useless" rather than "completely useless" is that if the text of your form gives a poor score on a readability test, then you definitely have a problem. However, getting a good score tells you nothing.

Appearance

Lupton, E. (2004) *Thinking with type: A Critical Guide for Designers, Writers, Editors & Students.* New York: Princeton Architectural Press.

> Beautiful short book. A superb introduction to the subtleties of typography.

Spiekermann, E., and Ginger, E. M. (1993) *Stop Stealing Sheep & Find Out How Type Works.* Mountain View, California: Adobe Press.

> Easy, interesting book on typography. Font-led, paper-oriented. Good for advice on choosing style of font and legibility. The book's form example has ambiguous prompted underlines, so don't copy it.

Williams, R. (1994) The Non-Designer's Design Book: Design and Typographic Principles for the Visual Novice. Berkely, California: Peachpit Press.

> A short book that helps the non-designer to get a feel for design; includes quizzes and exercises for you to try.

Elam, K. (2004) Grid Systems: Principles of Organizing Type. New York: Princeton Architectural Press.

> Another engaging book in the Princton Architectual Press series. This one deals with designing to a grid.

Ware, C. (2000) *Information Visualization: Perception for Design.* San Francisco: Morgan Kaufmann Publishers.

> Interesting chapter on color within scientific but readable textbook on visualization and perception.

Usability Testing

Dumas, J. S., and Redish, J. C. (1999) *A Practical Guide to Usability Testing*. Portland, Oregon: Intellect Books.

> Dumas and Redish is the standard text on usability testing. Practical, easy to read, easy to follow.

Rubin, J., and Chisnell, D. (2007) *Handbook of Usability Testing: How to Plan, Design and Conduct Effective Tests*. New York: John Wiley & Sons, Inc.

> A comprehensive, clear, and down-to-earth handbook of usability testing. Recently updated and issued in a new edition.

Snyder, C. (2007) *Paper Prototyping: The Fast and Easy Way to Design and Refine User Interfaces*. San Francisco: Morgan Kaufmann Publishers.

> Thorough and practical book on how to create and test paper protoypes.

Barnum, C. M. (2002) *Usability Testing and Research*. New York: Longman.

> Barnum's book sets usability testing in context and then takes you through planning, conducting, and reporting on a test. She uses a running example of a web usability test conducted by her students at Southern Polytechnic State University, so it is easy to see how to apply the techniques.

Professional associations

Society for Technical Communication (STC)
http://www.stc.org

> For technical communicators. Has a strong usability and user experience special interest group and an excellent, very readable but authoritative journal that frequently contains articles on usability and information design.

Usability Professionals' Association (UPA)
http://www.usabilityprofessionals.org

> For usability practitioners and people interested in usability as part of their work.

Business Forms Management Association (BFMA)
http://www.bfma.org

> Originally for people who manage forms, but increasingly also of interest if you design forms. Essential if you are trying to control a large number of forms.

Print Services & Distribution Association (PSDA)
http://www.psda.org/

> Formerly the Document Management Industries Association (DMIA). PSDA is *the* resource if you need to learn about the manufacture of paper forms. Look in the "Education" section, then "Catalog" for their books and other resources. For example, this is where to come if you need to learn about printing multipart forms with tear-off sections.

Clarity
http://www.clarity-international.net

> The lawyers' association for plain language, also open to non-lawyers. Publishes an interesting journal and has remarkably low dues.

References

Bartell, A. L., Schultz, L. D., and Spyridakis, J. H. (2006) "The Effect of Heading Frequency on Comprehension of Print Versus Online Information." *Technical Communication*, *53*(4): 416–426.

Burnside, R., Bishop, G., and Guiver, T. (2005) "The Effect of an Incentive on Response Rates and Timing in an Economic Survey." Retrieved May 22 2008 from http://www.oecd.org/dataoecd/24/51/34976200.pdf

Dillman, D. A. (2000) *Mail and Internet Surveys: The Tailored Design Method*. New York: John Wiley & Sons Inc.

Dixon, P. (1987) "The Processing of Organizational and Component Step Information in Written Directions." *Journal of Memory and Language*, *26*: 24–35.

Fogg, B. J. (2002) "Stanford Guidelines for Web Credibility." A Research Summary from the Stanford Persuasive Technology Lab. Stanford University. Retrieved May 22 2008 from www.webcredibility.org/guidelines

Hackos, J. T., and Redish, J. C. (1998) *User and Task Analysis for Interface Design*. New York: John Wiley and Sons, Inc.

Hoffmann, D. E., Zimmerman, S. I., and Tompkins, C. J. (1996) "The Dangers of Directives or the False Security of Forms." *Journal of Law, Medicine & Ethics*, *24*(1): 5–17.

James, J. M., and Bolstein, R. (1992) "Large Monetary Incentives and Their Effect on Mail Survey Response Rates." *Public Opinion Quarterly*, *56*: 442–453.

Jarrett, C. (2000) *Designing usable forms: the three layer model of the form*. Proceedings of the Society for Technical Communication Conference. Orlando, Florida.

Jarrett, C., and Quesenbery, W. (2006) *How to Look at a Form—in a Hurry*. Proceedings of the Usability Professionals' Association Conference. Minneapolis, Minnesota.

Karvonen, K. (2000) *The Beauty of Simplicity.* Proceedings of the Conference on Universal Usability, ACM. Arlington, Virginia.

Nielsen, J., and Landauer, T. K. (1993) "A Mathematical Model of the Finding of Usability Problems." *Proceedings of INTERCHI, 93*: 206–213.

Penzo, M. (2006) *Label Placement in Forms.* Retrieved May 22 2008 from www.uxmatters.com/MT/archives/000107.php

Redish, J. C. (Ginny) (2007) *Letting Go of the Words: Writing Web Content That Works*, San Francisco: Morgan Kaufmann.

Quesenbery, W. (2006) "Personas and Narrative." In Pruitt., J. and Adlin, T. (Eds). *The Persona Lifecycle*, pp. 520–554. San Francisco: Morgan Kauffman.

Tourangeau, R., Rips, L. J., and Rasinski, K. (2000) *The Psychology of Survey Response.* New York: Cambridge University Press.

Wroblewski, L. (2008) *Web Form Design: Filling in the Blanks.* Brooklyn, New York: Rosenfeld Media.

Index